Hiking & Biking
the
I&M Canal National Heritage Corridor

An American Bike Trails Publication

Hiking & Biking
the
I&M Canal
National Heritage Corridor

Published by	American Bike Trails
Copyright 2006 by	American Bike Trails
Created by	Ray Hoven
Illustrated & Designed by	Mary C. Rumpsa

Cover photo by Larry Kane and courtesy of Canal Corridor Association

All Rights Reserved. Reproduction of any part of this book in any form without written permission is prohibited.

American Bike Trails assumes no responsibility or liability for any person or entity with respect to injury or damage caused either directly or indirectly by the information contained in this book.

Table of Contents

Acknowledgements 5
Explanation of Terms 6
Explanation of Symbols 8
Health Hazards 9
Tips for Bicyclists 11
Trail Statistics 12
I & M Canal Corridor History 14
I & M Canal Corridor 18

Section 1
I & M Canal Corridor 20
Chicago Lakefront Bike Path 22
Cook County I&M Bicycle Trail 26
Salt Creek Greenway 28
Salt Creek Forest Preserve 30
Bemis Woods 32
Wolf Road Prairie 34
Arie Crown Forest Preserve & Trail 36
Palos & Sag Valley Forest Preserves 38
Lake Katherine Nature Preserve 44
Waterfall Glen Forest Preserve 46
Lemont's I&M Canal Walk Heritage Quarries Recreation Area 51
Black Partridge Forest Preserve 54

Section 2
Forest Preserve District of Will County Biking Trails 55
Will County's Linear Trails 58
Old Plank Road Trail 61
Wauponsee Glacial Trail 64
Rock Run Trail & the Joliet Trail Loop 66
Rock Run Preserve Black Road Access and Nichols Access 68
Rock Run Preserve Theodore Marsh 69
Will County I&M Canal Trail 70
Centennial Trail (under development) 72

Section 3
Northwestern Will County 75
Gaylord Donnelley Canal Trail 76
O'Hara Woods Nature Preserve 78
Keepataw Preserve 79
Veterans Woods 79
Lake Renwick Preserve – Turtle Lake Access/Lake Renwick Bikeway 80
Lake Renwick – Heron Rookery Nature Preserve 80
Lockport Prairie Nature Preserve 84
Joliet Iron Works Historic Site 86
Pilcher Park 88
Hammel Woods/Hammel Woods Bikeway 90
Sugar Creek Preserve 92

Table of Contents (continued)

Section 4
Southwestern Will County 93
McKinley Woods 94
Braidwood Dunes & Savanna Nature Preserve 96
Forsythe Woods 98
Channahon State Park 100
Midewin National Tallgrass Prairie 102
Kankakee River State Park 104

Section 5
Central & Eastern Will County 106
Spring Creek Preserve – Homer Trails 108
Messenger Woods 110
Hickory Creek Preserve/Bikeway East Branch and West Branch 112
Hickory Creek Preserve/Bikeway West Branch 114
Hickory Creek Preserve/Bikeway East Branch 115
Monee Reservoir 116
Raccoon Grove Forest Preserve 118
Thorn Creek Woods Nature Preserve 120
Goodenow Grove Nature Preserve 122

Section 6
The Illinois & Michigan Canal State Trail and nearby parks 124
The Illinois and Michigan Canal State Trail 126
Goose Lake Prairie State Natural Area 136
Gebhard Woods State Park 138
Buffalo Rock State Park 140
Illini State Park 142
Starved Rock State Park 144
Matthiessen State Park 150
Catlin Park 152

Section 7
Interconnections 154
Grand Illinois Trail 155
Kaskaskia-Alliance Trail (under development) 158
Hennepin Canal State Parkway 160

Indexes
Visitors Centers 164
Accommodations 165
Organizations 168
City to Trail Index 170
County to Trail Index 172
Trail Index 174

Acknowledgements

We greatly appreciate the support, input, and guidance provided by the many professionals who contributed to the development of this book.

Adele Hoddi	Illinois Dept. of Natural Resources
Bruce Hodgdon	Forest Preserve District of Will County
Dave Kircher	Forest Preserve District of Cook County
Ana Koval	I&M Canal Corridor Association
Glenn P. Knoblock	Forest Preserve District of Will County
Lynn Kurczewski	Forest Preserve District of Will County
Ron Vasile	I&M Canal Corridor Association
Rose Yates	Village of Lemont

Explanation of Terms

Bog	An acidic wetland that is fed by rainwater and is characterized by open water with a floating mat of vegetation (e.g. sedges, mosses, tamarack) that will often bounce if you jump on it.
Bluff	A high steep bank with a broad, flat, or rounded front.
Canyon	A deep narrow valley with precipitous side often with a stream flowing through it.
Drumlin	Smooth oval hill of glacial drift, elongated in the direction of the movement of the ice that deposited it. Drumlins may be more than 150 feet high and more than a half mile long.
Esker	A long winding, serpentine ridge of glacial drift (gravel) with steep sides (10-50 feet high).
Fen	An alkaline wetland that is fed by ground water and is often seen as a wet meadow and characterized by plants like Grass or Parnasis and sedges that grow in alkaline water.
Forest	A vegetative community dominated by trees and many containing understory layers of smaller trees, shorter shrubs and an herbaceous layers at the ground.
Grove	A small wooded area without underbrush, such as a picnic area.
Herb	A seed producing annual, biennial, or perennial that does not develop persistent woody tissue but dies down at the end of a growing season.
Kame	An oval depression of glacial till, often filled with water, formed when buried and stranded chunks of ice from a retreating glacier melted.
Kettle	Oval depression found in glacial moraines, which are landforms made up of rock debris, melts, as the ground above it subsides, forming a kettle.
Lake	A considerable inland body of standing water.
Marsh	A wetland fed by streams and with shallow or deep water. Often characterized by mats of cattail, bulrushes, sedges and wetland forbs.
Mesic	A type of plant that requires a moderate amount of water.
Moraine	Long, irregular hills of glacial till deposited by stagnant and retreating glaciers.

Natural Community	A group of living organisms that live in the same place, e.g. woodland or prairie.
Park	An area maintained in its natural state as a public property.
Pond	A body of water usually smaller than a lake.
Prairie	Primarily treeless grassland community characterized by full sun and dominated by perennial, native grasses and forbs. Isolated remnants of tall grass prairie can be found in southeastern portions of the greater Milwaukee area.
Preserve	An area restricted for the protection and preservation of natural resources.
Ridge	A range of hills or mountains.
Savanna	A grassland ecosystem with scattered trees (predominantly bur oak in southeastern Wisconsin) characterized by native grasses and forbs.
Sedges	Grass-like plants with triangular stems and without showy flowers. Many are dominant in sedge meadows, bogs and fens but others are found in woodlands or prairies.
Shrubs	Low woody plants, usually shorter than trees and with several stems.
Swale	A lower lying or depressed and off wet stretch of land.
Swamp	Spongy land saturated and sometimes partially or intermittently covered with water.
Turf	The upper stratum of soil bound by grass and plant roots into a thick mat.
Wetland	The low lying wet area between higher ridges.

Explanation of Symbols

SYMBOL LEGEND

- Beach/Swimming
- Bicycle Repair
- Cabin
- Camping
- Canoe Launch
- First Aid
- Food
- Golf Course
- Information
- Lodging
- Multi-Facilities
- Parking
- Picnic
- Ranger Station
- Restrooms
- Shelter
- Trailhead
- Visitor Center
- Water
- Overlook/Observation

AREA LEGEND

- City, Town
- Parks, Preserves
- Waterway
- Marsh/Wetland
- Mileage Scale
- Points of Interest
- County/State
- Forest/Woods

TRAIL LEGEND

- Trail-Biking/Multi
- Skiing only Trail
- Hiking only Trail
- Planned Trail
- Alternate Trail
- Road/Highway
- Railroad Tracks

Health Hazards

Hypothermia

Hypothermia is a condition where the core body temperature falls below 90 degrees. This may cause death.

Mild hypothermia
1. Symptoms
   a. Pronounced shivering
   b. Loss of physical coordination
   c. Thinking becomes cloudy
2. Causes
   a. Cold, wet, loss of body heat, wind
3. Treatment
   a. Prevent further heat loss, get out of wet clothing and out of wind. Replace wet clothing with dry.
   b. Help body generate more heat. Refuel with high-energy foods and a hot drink, get moving around, light exercise, or external heat.

Severe hypothermia
1. Symptoms
   a. Shivering stops, pulse and respiration slows down, speech becomes incoherent.
2. Treatment
   a. Get help immediately.
   b. Don't give food or water.
   c. Don't try to rewarm the victim in the field.
   d. A buildup of toxic wastes and tactic acid accumulates in the blood in the body's extremities. Movement or rough handling will cause a flow of the blood from the extremities to the heart. This polluted blood can send the heart into ventricular fibrillations (heart attach). This may result in death.
   e. Wrap victim in several sleeping bags and insulate from the ground.

Frostbite

Symptoms of frostbite may include red skin with white blotches due to lack of circulation. Rewarm body part gently. Do not immerse in hot water or rub to restore circulation, as both will destroy skin cell.

Health Hazards (continued)

Heat Exhaustion

Cool, pale, and moist skin, heavy sweating, headache, nausea, dizziness and vomiting. Body temperature nearly normal.

Treatment	Have victim lie in the coolest place available– on back with feet raised. Rub body gently with cool, wet cloth. Give person ½ glass of water every 15 minutes if conscious and can tolerate it. Call for emergency medical assistance.

Heat Stroke

Hot, red skin, shock or unconsciousness; high body temperature.

Treatment	Treat as a life-threatening emergency. Call for emergency medical assistance immediately. Cool victim by any means possible. Cool bath, pour cool water over body, or wrap wet sheets around body. Give nothing by mouth.

West Nile Virus

West Nile Virus is transmitted by certain types of mosquitoes. Most people infected with West Nile Virus won't develop symptoms. Some may become ill 3 to 15 days after being bitten.

Protect Yourself	Wear property clothing, use insect repellents and time your outdoor activities to reduce your risk of mosquito bites and other insect problems. Most backyard mosquito problems are caused by mosquitoes breeding in and around homes, not those from more natural areas.

Tips for Bicyclists

- Pushing in gears that are too high can push knees beyond their limits. Avoid extremes by pedaling faster rather than shifting into a higher gear.

- Keeping your elbows bent, changing your hand position frequently and wearing bicycle gloves all help to reduce the numbness or pain in the palm of the hand from long-distance riding.

- Keep you pedal rpms up on an uphill so you have reserve power if you lose speed.

- Stay in a high-gear on a level surface, placing pressure on the pedals and resting on the handle bars and saddle.

- Lower your center of gravity on a long or steep downhill run by using the quick release seat post binder and dropping the saddle height down.

- Brake intermittently on a rough surface.

- Wear proper equipment. Wear a helmet that is approved by the Snell Memorial Foundation or the American National Standards Institute. Look for one of their stickers inside the helmet.

- Use a lower tire inflation pressure for riding on unpaved surfaces. The lower pressure will provide better tire traction and a more comfortable ride.

- Apply your brakes gradually to maintain control on loose gravel or soil.

- Ride only on trails designated for bicycles or in areas where you have the permission of the landowner.

- Be courteous to hikers or horseback riders on the trail, they have the right of way.

- Leave riding trails in the condition you found them. Be sensitive to the environment. Properly dispose of your trash. If you open a gate, close it behind you.

- Don't carry items or attach anything to your bicycle that might hinder your vision or control.

- Don't wear anything that restricts your hearing.

- Don't carry extra clothing where it can hang down and jam in a wheel.

Trail Statistics

Park, Preserve or Trail	Miles Hike	Miles Bike	Surface
Arie Crown Forest Preserve	3.2	3.2	Crushed gravel
Bemis Woods	3.0	3.0	Packed earth
Black Partridge Forest Preserve	0.5	-	Packed earth
Braidwood Dunes&Savanna NP	1.5	-	Natural
Buffalo Rock State Park	2.5	-	Gravel
Catlin Park	13.0	13.0	Mowed turf, packed earth
Centennial Trail	20.0	20.0	(A planned trail - crushed stone)
Chicago Lakefront Bike Path	20.0	20.0	Asphalt
Cook County I&M Bicycle Trail	8.9	8.9	Paved
Forsythe Woods	2.0	-	Natural
Gaylord Donneley Canal Trail	2.5	2.5	Asphalt, limestone screenings
Gebhard Woods State Park			Natural, Length undermined
Goodenow Grove Nature Prsrv	3.5	-	Paved, gravel, natural
Goose Lake Prairie State NA	7.0	-	Natural
Grand Illinois Trail	500+	500+	Multiple surfaces
Hammel Woods	3.0	3.0	Limestone screenings, natural
Hennepin Canal Parkway	98.0	98.0	Bituminous – 2 miles, oil & chip – miles, gravel 35 mi.
Hickory Creek Preserve	3.6	3.6	Asphalt, packed earth
I&M Canal State Trail	61.5	61.5	Limestone screenings
Illini State Park	2.0		
Joliet Junction Trail	4.4	4.4	Paved
Kankakee River State Park	10.5	10.5	Limestone screenings
Kaskaskia-Alliance Trail	15.0	15.0	(planned)
Keepataw Preserve	.3	-	Mowed turf
Lake Katherine Nature Preserve	3.5	-	Mowed turf, woodchips
Lake Renwick Preserve	2.9	-	Natural

Park, Preserve or Trail	Miles		Surface
	Hike	Bike	
Lemont's I&M Canal Trail	6.8	6.8	Crushed limestone
Lockport Prairie Nature Preserve	.4		Packed earth
Matthiessen State Park	5.0	5.0	Gravel, natural
McKinley Woods	2.5	-	Packed earth
Messenger Woods Nature Preserve	2.0	-	Packed earth
Midewin National Tallgrass Prairie	13.0	13.0	Old roads
Monee Reservoir	2.5	-	Mowed turf
O'Hara Woods Nature Preserve	3.0	-	Packed earth
Old Plank Road Trail	21.0	21.0	Asphalt
Palos & Sag Forest Preserve Trails	32.0	32.0	Natural/groomed
Pilcher Park	5.0	3.0	Asphalt & gravel – 3 miles, woodchip – 2 miles
Raccoon Grove Nature Preserve	.5	-	Packed earth
Rock Run Prairie	9.0	9.0	Asphalt
Salt Creek Greenway & FP	6.6	6.6	Asphalt
Spring Creek Greenway Homer Trails	3.2	-	Limestone, mowed turf, packed earth
Starved Rock State Park	13.0	-	Natural
Thorn Creek Woods Nature Preserve	2.5	-	Packed earth
Veterans Woods	.35	-	Packed earth
Waterfall Glen Forest Preserve	11.7	11.7	Limestone screenings
Wauponsee Trail	23.6	23.6	Asphalt 3.3 miles, limestone screenings - 20.3 miles
Will County I&M Canal Trail	11.4	11.4	Asphalt, limestone screenings
Wolf Road Prairie	.2		Packed earth

I & M Canal Corridor History

The opening of the Illinois &Michigan Canal ushered in a new era in trade and travel for the nation. By connecting the waters of the Illinois River with those of Lake Michigan (hence the name, hereafter referred to as the I&M Canal), the canal created an all-water route from New York to New Orleans, with Chicago as the crucial mid-point. The I&M Canal, opened 23 years after the Erie Canal, was the last of the great U. S. shipping canals of the nineteenth century. Following up on the Erie's success, the I&M was the final link in a chain of waterways that helped fuel the nation's economic growth.

In 1673, Louis Jolliet and Father Jacques Marquette were the first Europeans to venture into the area. They and their company were returning to Canada from their explorations down the Mississippi River.

Marquette and Jolliet had traveled north from the Mississippi by way of the Illinois and Des Plaines Rivers. At a point now known as the Chicago Portage, they encountered a low divide that separated them from the Chicago River and Lake Michigan. Jolliet early on saw the opportunity of providing an uninterrupted route to the Gulf of Mexico. He wrote that if a short canal were dug through the portage, one could travel from Lake Michigan to the Gulf entirely by boat.

The French continued to control the region until their defeat by the British in the French and Indian War. After the American Revolution, the American government negotiated a treaty with the Potawatomi tribe, in which the Potawatomi ceded six square miles of land at the mouth of the Chicago River. Part of this area became the site of Fort Dearborn.

Interest in a canal began to increase in the early 1800's, and in 1816, the Potawatomi ceded land ten miles on either side of the Des Plaines and Illinois Rivers from Lake Michigan to the Fox River. In 1823 Illinois created a Canal Commission, but progress was limited by the lack of financial resources. In 1835 a new Canal Commission was formed and, unlike the first, it was empowered to raise money.

The Commission had a federal grant of 284,000 acres of land along the proposed canal route, which it tried to sell for $1.25 an acre to fund construction. Land sales were difficult, but enough funds were raised to start canal construction on Independence Day, 1836. Construction proceeded stop-and-go, but after a four year stoppage, new funding was secured from English and eastern investors and the Illinois and Michigan Canal was officially opened its locks in 1848.

Chief Engineer William Gooding was put in charge of engineering and construction. His plan divided the Canal into three sections: The Summit segment (Chicago to Lockport), the Middle segment (Lockport to Seneca), and the Western segment (Seneca to LaSalle). The Canal was to be 60 feet wide at water level, 36 feet wide at the bottom, and six feet deep along its entire 96 mile length. The Canal connected to Lake Michigan via 4.5 miles of the Chicago River. A total of 17 locks were built on the Canal. These locks were needed to lift or lower boats along the course of the Canal as water levels changes. Other construction included aqueducts to carry the Canal over rivers and streams, bridges, dams, lockkeepers' houses and the towpath along which mules pulled the canal boats.

History (continued)

For the first time, a cargo of sugar and other goods from New Orleans reached the docks of Buffalo, New York in April of 1848. From a trickle, the commerce between east and west swelled into a continuous flow of people and goods. Chicago became the Midwest's hub, and the city's population soared 600% in the decade after the opening of the Canal. The Chicago and Rock Island Railroad paralleled the canal by 1853 and took away the canal passenger trade. The canal held its own in competing with the railroads in the shipment of freight. Tolls reached a peak of over $300,000 in 1866, and tonnage topped out at over 1 million tons in 1881. The Canal's intense growth began to wane by the late 1880s, and beginning in 1871 the I&M carried sewage away from Chicago.

In 1900, the larger Sanitary and Ship Canal began operating, carrying both wastes and larger, more modern barges. All use of the I&M Canal ended in 1933, with the opening of the Canal's modern successor – the Illinois Waterway.

On August 24, 1984, President Ronald Reagan signed legislation establishing the region as the nation's first National Heritage Corridor. The I&M Canal National Heritage Corridor is a 100 mile long cultural park between Chicago and LaSalle/Peru. It contains roughly 322,000 acres within the counties of Cook, DuPage, Will, Grundy and LaSalle.

Canal Corridor Association

The Canal Corridor Association (CCA) is a nonprofit membership organization that creates destinations for learning and fun throughout the Illinois & Michigan Canal National Heritage Corridor.

The 65+ miles of recreational trails in the Heritage Corridor are among its most popular features. CCA is installing mile markers that feature tidbits of canal history, along with life-size sculptures of canal pioneers along the Heritage Corridor's trails to bring the early days of the historic, hand-dug canal to life. CCA also works with partners along the Heritage Corridor to create parks, protect nature and preserve history for visitors to enjoy. Visit www.canalcor.org to learn more about CCA and become a member.

Photo courtesy of the I&M Canal Heritage Association

I & M Canal Corridor

The I&M Canal Corridor embraces 450 square miles, encompasses forty-nine distinct communities, and spans portions of five counties (Cook, DuPage, Will, Grundy and LaSalle). Included in this 96 mile long stretch of the Illinois Valley are major cities such as Chicago and Joliet,

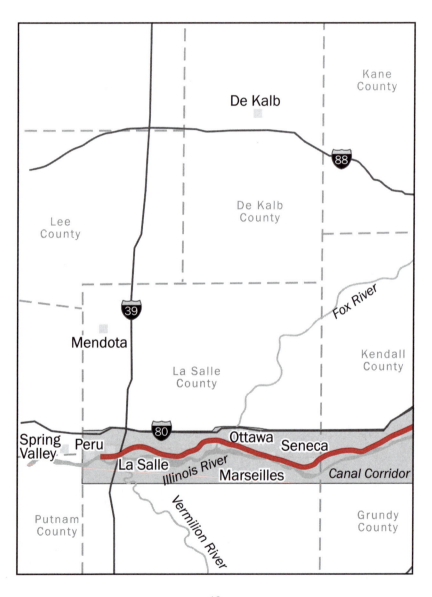

industrial enclaves such a Bedford Park and McCook, rural farms in the vicinity of Marseilles and Seneca, and coal town such as Carbon Hill and Coal City.

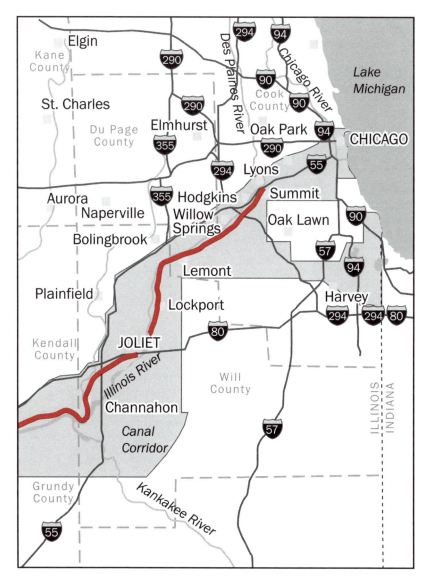

I & M Canal Corridor – Section 1

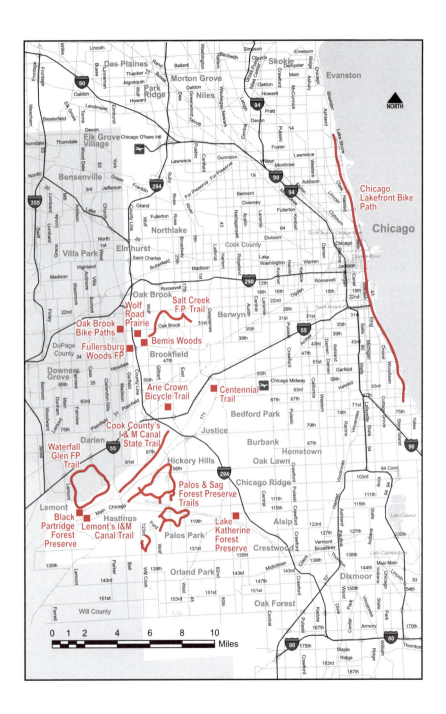

Bike riding on the Chicago lakefront

Photo courtesy of Brook Collins/ Chicago Park District

Chicago Lakefront Bike Path

Trail Length	Approximately 20 miles
Surface	Paved
Information	Chicago Park District 312-747-2200
County	Cook

The symbolic starting point for a venture through the National Historic Corridor is Navy Pier in downtown Chicago. By bike or foot, you can arrive at the Pier by taking the Chicago Lakefront Bike Path. The Path offers great views of Lake Michigan and the Chicago Skyline. From the north, the bike path begins around Bryn Mawr (5600 north) and Sheridan Road, and then proceeds south along the shoreline to 71st Street. By motor vehicle take Lake Shore Drive, north of the loop to Illinois Street. Head east on Illinois Street to the parking area at Navy Pier. Restaurants, tour boats, and many other amusements await the visitor. Plenty of bike racks are available.

Navy Pier was built in 1926, and was envisioned as a recreational center for Chicagoans. The east end of the pier was the end of the line for the Grand Avenue streetcar. Navy Pier was named as a memorial to Midwesterners who served in the U.S. Navy in World War 1. Nearby points of interest include the Oak Street Beach, the Chicago Historical Society, and the Chicago Academy of Sciences to the north, and Buckingham Fountain, the Field Museum of Natural History, and Shedd Aquarium to the south.

When Fort Dearborn was built in 1803, the Chicago River flowed into Lake Michigan a short distance south of what today is Navy Pier. It was fed by northern and southern branches that converge at Wolf Point (near the Merchandise Mart) the river headed east for one mile along present day Wacker Drive. As Chicago grew, more and more raw sewage and pollutants were conveniently dumped in the river, which then transported the mess into Lake Michigan. Since Chicago water comes from Lake Michigan, its citizens received part of the polluted liquids back in the form of drinking water. In 1900, the problem was tackled by the opening of the 28 mile Chicago Sanitary and Ship Canal, which reversed the flow of the Chicago River. It begins at Damen Avenue and the Stevenson Expressway (I-55) in Chicago, and runs in a southwesterly direction through the suburbs of Stickney, Forest View, Lyons, Summit, Bedford, Park, Justice, Willow Springs, Lemont, and Romeoville. The canal terminates in Lockport, where it joins the Des Plaines River. The northern end of the canal joins the South Branch of the Chicago River. The average width of the channel is around 300 feet, and its 24 foot depth accommodates barge and other boat traffic.

The Friends of the Chicago River have produced a series of walking-tour brochures for the Chicago River Trail along or close to the waterway. Each brochure contains a map detailing a walking route for each section as well as historical information and item of interest along the river. You can call them at 312-939-0490 for more information about these walking tours and how to get the maps. Their web site is www.chicagoriver.org.

Chicago Lakefront Bike Path

Continued on next page

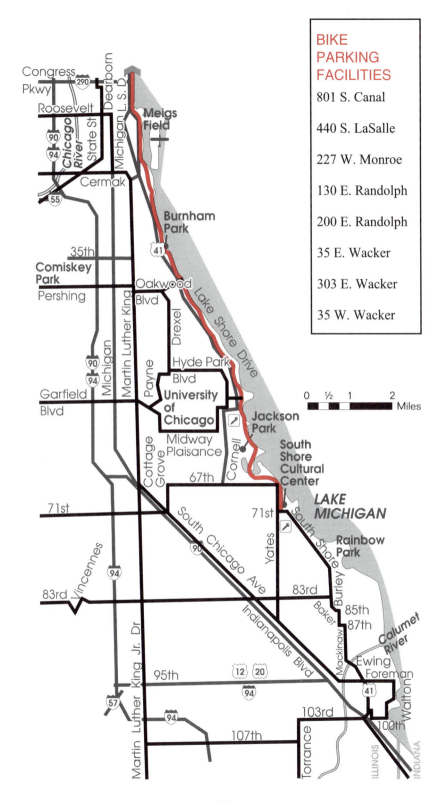

Cook County I&M Bicycle Trail

Trail Length	8.9 miles
Surface	Paved
Information	Palos Forest Preserve 708-361-1536
County	Cook

The paved I&M Canal Bicycle Trail is within the I&M Canal National Heritage Corridor. The 8.9 mile trail consists of three sections; two 3.3 mile loops and a 2.3 mile section that connects the two. From the parking area the trail heads northeast and southwest. Heading northeast, the asphalt trail leads through mature woods providing a shady and peaceful ride with little traffic sounds until you approach the I-194 underpass 1.6 miles out. Just past the interstate, the trail then heads back southwest paralleling the Chicago Sanitary and Ship Canal. Going southwest from the parking lot, you'll notice that soil and vegetation have filled in the canal. At the intersection 2.3 miles out from the parking lot trailhead is the other 3.3 mile loop along the canal. Taking the trail to the right takes you past two railroad crossings as well as a chemical company entrance. The trail ends at the Route 83 overpass and then loops back northeast.

Getting There   Take Route 83 south of the Des Plaines River to Archer Avenue, then take Archer Avenue northwest of Willow Springs Road for .2 miles. Turn left on Market Street where you will see a large bicycle trail welcome sign. Continue for .2 miles through an industrial area. Cross under the Willow Springs Road bridge and over the Metra railroad tracks to the first parking lot.

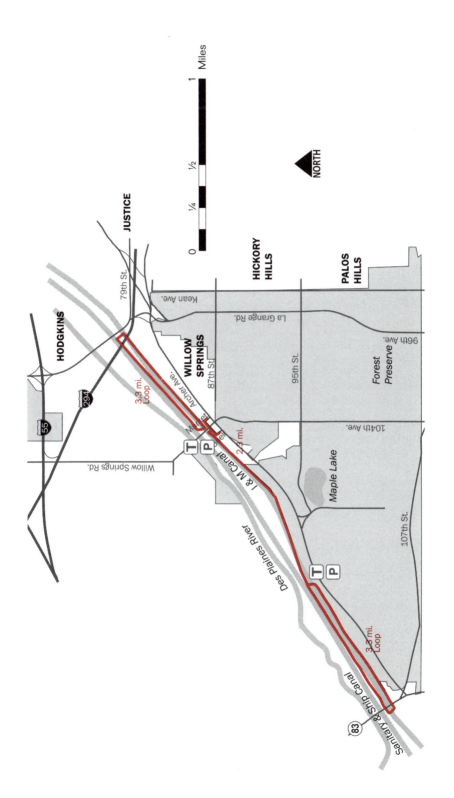

Salt Creek Greenway

Salt Creek runs through northwestern Cook County, then flows south to DuPage County before heading back east into central Cook County where it empties into the Des Plaines River south of Brookfield. The Salt Creek has several forest preserves along it's shores providing habitat for wildlife. There are also many trails in these forest preserves and communities along the creek.

There is no salt water in the creek today, but there is a story that the name Salt Creek came from a 19th century farmer's mishap. His wagon, loaded with salt barrels, got stuck in the water during a crossing. The next day he discovered the salt had washed into the creek, thus this misadventure continues to live on. By the 1970's, with all the development in the western suburbs, water quality had deteriorated badly. With the introduction of more effective sewage treatment and the establishment of natural area greenway surrounding the creek, water quality is much improved, and waterfowl and other wildlife have returned.

You'll find trails at three sites along the Salt Creek Greenway in central Cook County.

Salt Creek Forest Preserve

Trail Length	6.6 miles
Surface	Asphalt paved
Information	Forest Preserve District of Cook County 708-366-9420
County	Cook

Located in west central Cook County. Bordered clockwise by the communities of Oakbrook, Westchester, Brookfield, LaGrange Park, LaGrange, and Hinsdale. The Salt Creek starts in Bemis Woods South and continues east to Brookfield Woods, directly across from the Brookfield Zoo. As the trail follows Salt Creek, it provides access to various picnic groves and other points of interest. The trail is windy and has some hills. There are five road crossings and several forest preserves along the way. A new bridge across Salt Creek offers a scenic view with tree branches overhanging the creek. Narrow side trails head off along the creek and into the woods. Hugging the creek in spots, the trail runs mostly through mature woodlands.

For a side trip to the Brookfield Zoo, head east on 31st Street for .2 miles from the eastern trailhead at Brookfield Woods. The Forest Preserve District of Cook County owns and The Chicago Zoological Society operates this world famous zoo. Here you can observe more than 2,500 animals of 400 different species and enjoy a relaxing walk. For hours and admission prices call 708-485-0263.

Getting There   The trail may be accessed from Ogden Avenue, just east of Wolf Road, or from 31st Street between 1st Avenue and Prairie Avenue.

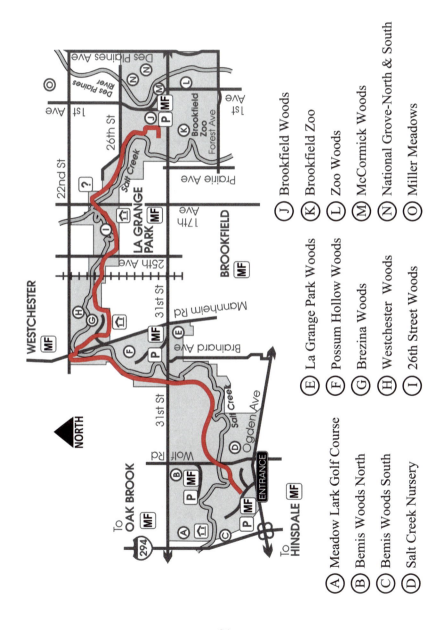

Bemis Woods

Trail Length	3 miles
Surface	Packed earth
Information	Forest Preserve District of Cook County 708-771-1330
County	Cook

This a is 3 mile unpaved, multi-use trail running through the gently rolling terrain by Salt Creek in Bemis Woods Preserve north of Western Springs. The western trailhead for the Salt Creek Bicycle Trail is also here. The trail loops through hilly woodland and along the meandering creek. The surface is packed earth or loose gravel in some spots. The path is mostly 8 to 10 feet wide but narrows to a single track overgrown with vegetation in some spots. It's easy to lose your way with all the trail intersections. Bemis Woods is open to hikers, bicyclists and equestrians.

Getting There   Take Ogden Avenue (Route 34) .5 mile east of I-294. The entrance is to the north. There is a second entrance a bit farther east off of Wolf Road .6 miles north of Ogden. Both entrance provide easy access to the multi-use trail.

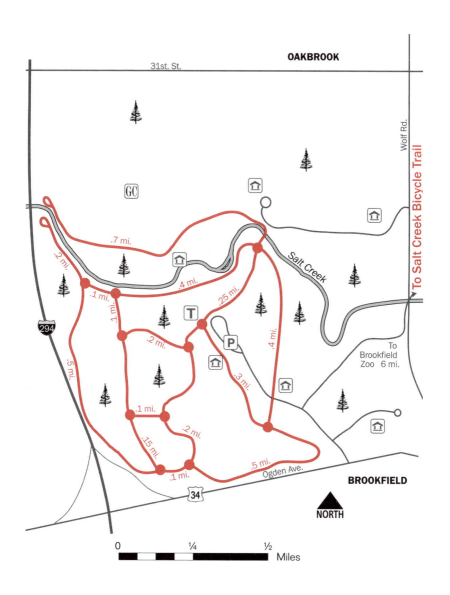

Wolf Road Prairie

Trail Length	2 miles
Surface	1.5 miles sidewalk, .5 mile mowed turf
Information	Forest Preserve District of Cook County 708-771-1330
County	Cook

Wolf Road Prairie is an excellent example of the original tallgrass prairie of Illinois and is the largest prairie of its type remaining in the Chicago area. Recognized as the finest and largest silt loam soil prairie east of the Mississippi River, and it is incredibly diverse. The prairie is dominated by big bluestem, little bluestem, prairie dropseed and Indian grass. A marsh dominated by bulrush and cattail and a small savanna remnant also occur here. The savanna is dominated by bur oak with wild hyacinth, groundnut and meadow rue beneath the trees. Western chorus frog, fox snake, common snipe and swamp sparrow are some of the animals that occupy this preserve.

In the 1920s, developers designated this 80 acre site for residential development. It was the Great Depression that brought this development plan to a halt. Also the wetlands here made the site ill-suited for growing crops or grazing animals. Today the only surviving "development" is a grid of paired sidewalks that crisscross the southern half of the preserve.

You'll find no facilities here, so bring your own water. The Wolf Road Prairie is preserved by a consortium consisting of an active volunteer group called Save the Prairie Society, the Illinois Dept. of Natural Resources, the Forest Preserve District of Cook County, and the Illinois Nature Preserves Commission. Monthly Ecotours and special events are held throughout the year covering various conservation topics.

Getting There   Take Ogden Avenue east of I-294 past Bemis Woods Forest Preserve to Wolf Road. Head north on Wolf Road to 31st Street, then west (left) on 31st Street for .1 mile. There are three small concrete parking areas north of 31st Street. The pathway near the entrance is a set of rectangular grids of concrete connected with narrow earthen footpaths. The path to the right takes you to an information signpost and a 260 year old bur oak tree. The tree serves as an excellent example of its species whole thick, resilient bark survived the frequent fires that swept through and rejuvenated the area.

White Oak

Arie Crown Forest Preserve & Trail

Trail Length	3.2 miles
Surface	Crushed gravel
Information	Forest Preserve District of Cook County 708-366-9420
County	Cook

The Arie Crown Trail offers you a natural setting of gently rolling hills as it winds through the scenic Arie Crown Forest near Hodgkins. Wildflowers and many other native plants adorn the trail's edge, making it one of the more beautiful in the area. The trail is open from sunrise to sunset. There are several loops and trail intersections, so it is easy to get lost. There are a few hills to climb, a small creek to cross, and nearby Lake Ida to enjoy. The northern portion is quiet and peaceful, but traffic sounds increase as you approach I-55 to the south. Facilities include restrooms, water pumps, and picnic tables near several of the parking areas.

Getting There The Arie Crown Forest Preserve is located just northwest of the Cook County I&M Canal near Countryside and the Stevenson Expressway (I-55). The preserve can be accessed at Brainard and Joliet Road or LaGrange/Mannheim Road, north of 67th Street.

SYMBOL LEGEND

- Beach/Swimming
- Bicycle Repair
- Cabin
- Camping
- Canoe Launch
- First Aid
- Food
- Golf Course
- Information
- Lodging
- MF Multi-Facilities
- P Parking
- Picnic
- Ranger Station
- Restrooms
- Shelter
- T Trailhead
- Visitor Center
- Water
- Overlook/Observation

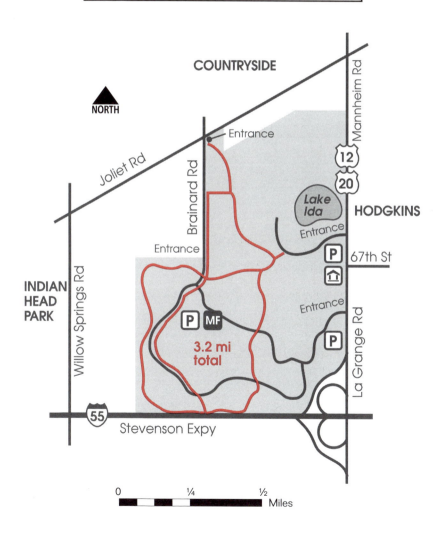

Palos & Sag Valley Forest Preserves

Trail Length	32 miles
Surface	Both natural & groomed
Information	Palos Forest Preserve 708-361-1536
County	Cook

Chicagoland's largest county forest preserve site. Palos and Sag Valley together encompass more than 14,000 acres of woods, prairie, and wetland in a hilly triangle with nine mile sides. You'll discover over 32 miles of unpaved, multi-use trails through the Palos Preserves as well as many miles of additional footpaths branching from the main trail. Two deep valleys slice between two high mounds of glacial debris, called moraines. Early settlers called the Palos Moraine in the north "Mount Forest Island", because its forested hills rose 150 feet above the flat prairie that stretched toward Lake Michigan. The trail network enables visitors to hike, bike and ski across miles of natural contours while avoiding most roads. It's a great way to appreciate the pockets of restored native habitat in the environment of a landscape that still needs much restoration attention. There are signposts at each intersection and color-coded wands every quarter mile, making it easier to stay on designated trails.

To get a sense of the glacial scale of these preserves, take a walk on the Ester Trail, a footpath looping up the southern moraine in the Cap Sauers Holdings, an Illinois Nature Preserve. From the top of the trail, the valley stretches out through the treetops to the Palos Moraine a mile away. Continuing along the esker's ridge, hikers will come to Visitation Prairie. This is as deep in wilderness as it gets in Cook County. Pause and listen to the landscape, silent of traffic, with only the soft rustle grass to break the stillness.

More than a century ago, Palos Hills farmers sent their children to school in a one room log cabin near what is now the busy intersection of 95th Street and La Grange Road. Classes continued until 1848. In 1952 the Forest Preserve District of Cook County converted the building to a nature center. Inside, visitors of all ages can peer inside tanks with field mice, turtles, and frogs, or observe busy bees perform intricate dances spinning in circles, moving forward and back. These dances give exact directions to where other bees can find flowers producing nectar they need to make their honey. Back outside, the White Oak and Black Oak footpaths offer one mile circuits through open woodlands. West of the schoolhouse is the 5.2 mile Palos Yellow Trail. The Yellow Trail head northeast to the high quality restored savanna of Spear Woods, where side-meanders skirt small sloughs and you may spot beaver and muskrat lodges.

The longest loop in the system is the eight mile Sag Valley Yellow Trail. Starting at the Swallow Cliff parking lot, the wide trail hugs the base of the bluff as it heads eastward. It eventually circles southwest to McClaughry Springs, an enchanting spot, especially in winter with its beautiful seeps. The Trail climbs to the top of the moraine above McClaughry, heading a mile west, where you can choose to weave through the Laughing Squaw Sloughs and continue west, or cut the trip short and head to the top of Swallow Cliff for a view across the Sag Valley, named for the former Saganashkee Swamp.

Palos & Sag Valley Forest Preserves (continued)

On the far west side of the Palos Preserves south of the Cal-Sag Channel you will find Camp Sagawau, open by reservation only. Here you can hike through Cook County's only natural rock canyon. Special programs include a canyon hike in which participants wade through a creek to enjoy the ferns, wildflowers, and rock formations. In spring, lush green ferns begin to unfold from closed fiddle-like branches to lacy green delights. Naturalists will also lead you on fossil hunts, and in the winter, you can participate in Nordic ski clinics. For more information on how to take a trip through this unique area call 630-257-2045.

At Tampier Lake you'll find another 4.5 miles of unpaved, multi-use trails south of McCarthy Road and west of Wolf Road. The .9 mile section south of Tampier Lake along 135th Street is relatively flat, bumpy, and not very interesting except for a nice view of the lake. The trail crosses Will-Cook Road and heads northwest through a large open field on a service road. North of 131st Street the trail becomes more interesting as it meanders through woods and open meadow before it dead ends at a slough.

Getting There   Due to the enormous size and scope of the Palos Preserves, parking locations are innumerable, but the following are recommended places to park that provide easy trail access to the nature centers and the multi-use trails. North of the Cal-Sag Channel, from the Willow Springs Road intersection with Archer Avenue south of the Des Plaines River, take Willow Springs south of 95th Street. Here Willow Springs becomes 104th Avenue. Proceed south. The Little Red Schoolhouse Nature Center entrance is on the west side. You can access the multi-use trail south of the parking lot where it intersects with the nature center path leading to the White Oak Trail.

Sag Valley Take Route 83 south to the Swallow Cliff Toboggan Slide entrance .2 miles west of 96th Avenue (Route 45).

Camp Sagawau Take Route 83 (111th Street) south of the Cal-Sag Channel and east of Archer Avenue. Proceed east for a short distance to the Camp Sagawau entrance on the north side of Route 83.

Tampier Lake Multi-Use Trail Take Will-Cook Road south of McCarthy Road and 131st Street to the Tampier Lake entrance .1 mile south of 131st Street on the east side.

Palos Forest Preserve (continued)

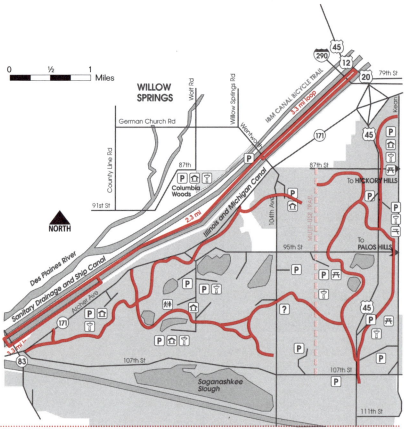

Match Line

SYMBOL LEGEND			
🏊	Beach/Swimming	MF	Multi-Facilities
🚲	Bicycle Repair	P	Parking
🏠	Cabin	⛱	Picnic
⛺	Camping	🏛	Ranger Station
🛶	Canoe Launch	🚻	Restrooms
+	First Aid	⛺	Shelter
🍴	Food	T	Trailhead
GC	Golf Course	🏛	Visitor Center
?	Information	🚰	Water
🛏	Lodging	🔭	Overlook/Observation

42

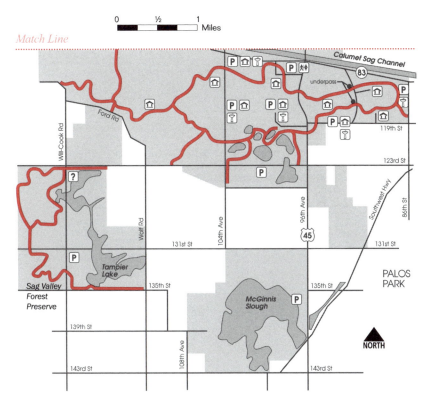

Lake Katherine Nature Preserve

Trail Length	3.5 miles
Surface	Woodchips, mowed turf
Information	Lake Katherine Nature Preserve 708-361-1873
County	Cook

Located in community of Palos Heights, this area along the Calumet-Sag Channel has been converted into a 158 acre nature preserve with a large lake, prairies, wetlands, a waterfall garden, and a Environmental Learning Center. Preserve visitors first encounter a picturesque waterfall and small rippling brook. Ducks swim in the pool at the bottom of the falls. Small conifers as well as flower and butterfly gardens are located nearby. In summer you may see hundreds of butterflies sipping nectar from annual and perennial flowers that have been planted there to attract them.

A walk on the 1 mile woodchip trail surrounding the 20 acre Lake Katherine leads to an overlook of the Calumet-Sag Channel and plantings of spruce, pine, and deciduous trees. At the western end of the lake is a short .5 mile trail through lowlands and a Children's Forest. On the east side of the lake is a nature center with displays as well as a children's theater. Educational programs are offered year round. East of the center is the Buzz N' Bloom Prairie containing many native prairie species. A trail through the prairie leads to a footbridge over a bubbling brook heading east to Harlem Avenue. There is an underpass at Harlem leading to the 33 acre Eastern Preserve with 2 miles of hiking trails through woods and prairie. After crossing under Harlem, you will encounter a massive waterfall flowing into the Cal-Sag Channel. The 2 miles of trail in the Eastern Preserve include a 1 mile woodchip path paralleling the channel called the Old Canoe Path Trail. A 1 mile Overlook Trail serves to complete a loop back to the nature center. This trail is rugged in spots with tree roots and loose rocks, and sometimes overgrown with vegetation.

Getting There   Located south of the Calumet-Sag Channel. You can take Route 83 east of Route 45 to 75th Avenue. The entrance is at the intersection of Route 83/College Drive and 75th Avenue/Lake Katherine Drive. If traveling by bike or foot you can take the asphalt paved Tinley Creek Bicycle Trail north from 131st Street for 2 miles to the preserve.

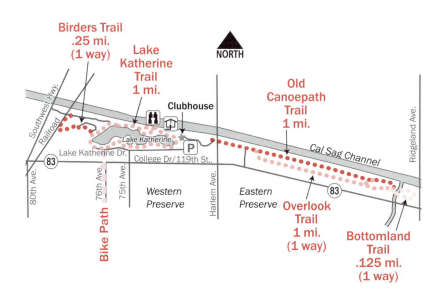

Waterfall Glen Forest Preserve

Trail Length	11.7 miles
Surface	Limestone screenings
Information	Forest Preserve District of DuPage County 630-933-7200
County	DuPage

Waterfall Glen is located in the southeast corner of DuPage County and encircles the Argonne National Laboratory. I-55 runs along the northern border and Route 83 near the eastern side. South of the trail is the conflux of the Santa Fe Railroad tracks, the Des Plaines River, the Chicago Sanitary and Ship Canal, and remnants of the historic I&M Canal.

Waterfall Glen provides some of the best bicycling, hiking and cross-country skiing in DuPage County. The main trail is 8 feet wide, and in

eastern bluebird

addition there are many grass trails and footpaths through the preserve. This is also one of DuPage County's most ecologically and scenically diverse areas. You'll find hilly ravines, rock outcroppings, a waterfall, and bluffs overlooking the Des Plaines River Valley. Living in this 2,470 acre ring of wilderness can be found the majority of plant species in DuPage County. Ten endangered plants and many plants of special concern grow here.

Argonne is one of the largest scientific research facilities in physical, biomedical, and environmental science, and in the development of energy sources of the future.

Getting There Take the Argonne National Laboratory/Cass Avenue exit (273A) off I-55 heading south on Cass, or take 91st Street 1.4 miles west of Route 83 to Cass Avenue heading north. Turn left at the Argonne National Laboratory visitor's sign. Follow the sign to the Waterfall Glen Ski-Equestrian Trailhead parking area.

Waterfall Glen Forest Preserve (continued)

Trail markers point out the main trail in both directions. Water and restroom are located at the trailhead, and at the Outdoor Education Camp area ¾ of the way around the preserve. If you are cycling, a mountain or hybrid bike may be preferable as the trail is very hilly with occasional rough spots. At 1.9 miles, you'll come to Westgate Road and an employee entrance into Argonne. Head west (right) along Westgate Road for .4 mile. At 3.3 miles out is a large slough where you can off sight wood ducks sitting on the half-submerged tree limbs.

At 3.8 miles, you'll come to a model airfield. On your left is the 80 acre Poverty Prairie named for the poverty oat grass that grows here along with mountain mint and pussytoes. To the right is the 200 acre Poverty Savannah with stately bur oaks. At 4.7 miles, the main trail climbs a hill to a "T" intersection. To the right along a service road is an information signpost and picnic area. You are now standing on top of a limestone bluff overlooking the Des Plaines River Valley to the south. In the late 19th and early 20th centuries, limestone quarries flourished in the river valley. In 1673, Louis Jolliet and Father Marquette canoed this area during their explorations. The service road leads out to South Bluff Road. To stay on the main trail follow the crushed limestone path to the left down the hill to the Santa Fe Railroad track.

Cross the service road at 5.5 miles out. Follow the trail marker straight ahead leading to a trail bridge over Saw Mill Creek. From 1860 to 1880, the Ward brothers operated a sawmill near here. To the east is Signal Hill where Native American communicated via smoke signals.

Heading back north brings you to the Rocky Glen and waterfall area. At 6.3 miles you'll come to a high bluff overlooking a creek below and a beautiful view. Be careful when near the edge, for there is a long drop to the creek bed below. After you pass the information signpost, take the first side trail to your left down to the waterfall, which was built by the Civilian Conservation Corps in the 1930s. This part of the trail is not open for biking.

At 6.7 miles, the main trail passes by the Outdoor Education Camp parking area off of Bluff Road. Cross over Bluff Road and continue north. As you head back west to complete the circle, you'll cross four more roads at the forest preserve maintenance center, 91st Street, Cass Avenue, and Northgate Road.

Waterfall Glen Forest Preserve (continued)

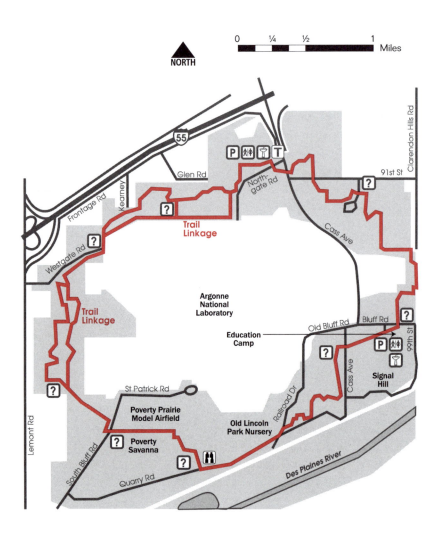

Lemont's I&M Canal Walk
Heritage Quarries Recreation Area

Trail Length	6.8 miles
Surface	Crushed limestone
Contact	Lemont Village Hall 630-257-1550
County	Cook

These trails run along the scenic banks of the I&M Canal. The trails feature spectacular natural views of the Canal and the Des Plaines Valley. They also serve as a link between Heritage Quarries Recreation Area and Lemont's Historic Downtown at General Fry's Landing. The Heritage Quarries Recreation Area adds an additional 3.8 mile trail extension to the existing 3 miles of trails along the original I&M Canal towpath. The trail extension weaves the Heritage Quarries into the original trail. Four pedestrian bridges provide access for hiking and biking in the nearly 300 acre natural area.

General Fry's Landing, named for the first canal boat to past through Lemont on the I&M Canal in 1848, is located in the heart of Lemont's downtown historic district. The Landing, a park and the I&M Canal interpretive center anchors the recreational trails to Lemont's downtown.

Lemont's Canal walk is a 3.5 miles linear multi-use path running along the I&M Canal in downtown Lemont south of the Chicago Sanitary and Ship Canal. At General Fry's Landing, a small park, you will find benches and a small Friendship Garden. There are no restrooms or water

Lemont's I&M Canal Walk & Heritage Quarries Recreation Area (continued)

fountains along the path, but several restaurants are located nearby. The walk is parallel but not part of the Centennial Trail.

Getting There   Take Lemont Road south of I-55 into downtown Lemont. Head east on Illinois Street to Stephen Street. Turn left (north) for three blocks after crossing the I&M Canal to the trail access. Trail parking is available along the canal near the Water Reclamation Plant.

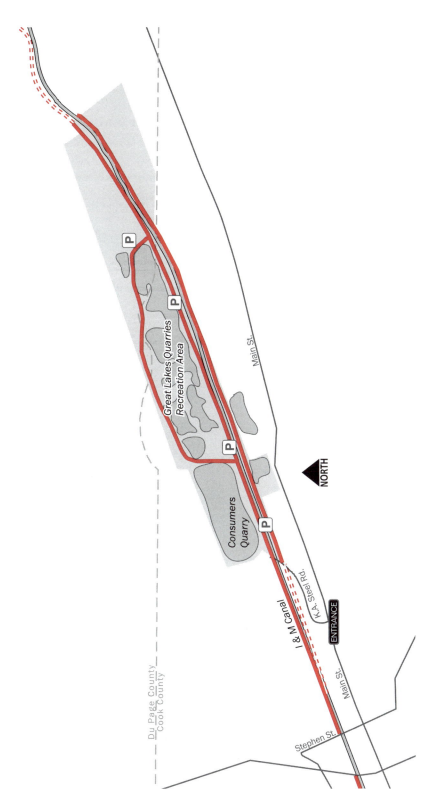

Black Partridge Forest Preserve

Trail Length	0.5 mile
Surface	Packed earth
Information	Forest Preserve District of Cook County 708-771-1330
County	Cook

Named for the Potawatomi Indian chief Black Partridge, this 80 acre preserve was dedicated in 1965 to protect its spring fed system. A dense tree canopy, interspersed with several small clearings, covers the majority of the preserve. The trails at Black Partridge are challenging with many steep and winding ravines. It borders the Sanitary Drainage and Ship Canal on the north. The mesic forest are dominated by sugar maple, basswood, red oak, and white oak, while the seep springs support skunk cabbage, marsh marigold, and a wide variety of wildflowers. Common animal species in the preserve include woodcock, gray squirrel, wood pewee, and redheaded woodpecker.

Getting There   From I-55, exit at Lemont Road. Proceed south on Lemont Road to 111th Street (Bluff road), then left (west) for one mile. The preserve is on the right.

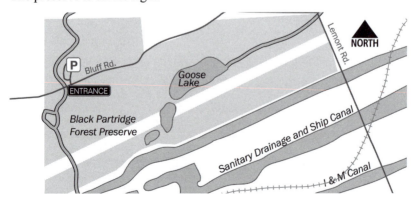

Forest Preserve District of Will County Biking Trails – Section 2

The opening of the Old Plank Road Trail (OPRT) in 1999 marked a milestone for the Forest Preserve District of Will County in recreational trail development. It had been twenty years since an abandoned rail line that ran through the center of the county was first recognized as being ideal for conversion to a regional trail—one that ran through a number of communities. The Old Plank Road Trail Commission was formed with representatives from all of the entities involved in the trail—the Village of Park Forest, the Illinois Department of Natural Resources, Rich Township, the Village of Frankfort, the Village of Matteson, and the Forest Preserve District of Will County. All of the communities that the 20 mile trail would run through, from Joliet to Park Forest in Cook County, had to be on board, an effort that required countless meetings and many delays.

Prior to the opening of the OPRT, trails created and managed by the Forest Preserve District were within the preserves themselves, and most focused on hiking. Regional trails, on the other hand, because of their extensive length, would provide recreation to bicyclists and most are therefore composed of asphalt.

The immediate popularity of the OPRT—to this day, the Village of Frankfort holds an annual celebration of this trail, and the Village of New Lenox is attempting to connect all of its neighborhoods to the trail with its own trail extensions—led to the acceptance of regional trails by municipalities.

Forest Preserve District of Will County Biking Trails (continued)

In the years since, the Forest Preserve District has built four additional regional trails, with a fifth partially completed at the time of this writing. Regional trails are now available in the Joliet area, with the Rock Run Greenway Trail and the Joliet Junction Trail; the Hickory Creek Bikeway, in Frankfort, Mokena and New Lenox; and the I & M Canal Trail, which runs from Joliet to Lockport to Romeoville. The Wauponsee Glacial Trail, from Joliet to the Kankakee River is under construction and should be completed in 2006. The Hammel Woods Bikeway, in Shorewood, is one link the proposed DuPage River Trail, which will follow the river from Shorewood into DuPage County and is a partnership of a number of government agencies.

Trail development will continue to be a major focus of future Forest Preserve District of Will County projects. Passage of another referendum by Will County voters in the spring of 2005, this one for $95 million, will provide funds for trail systems in the Naperville/Bolingbrook area and on the eastern end of the county. With the population exploding in the county, providing a nearby, scenic, and safe trail is an important goal of the District.

Preserve Hours

April through October	8:00 am – 8 pm
November through March	8:00 am – 5 pm

Trail Hours

Select preserves are open dawn to dusk to provide access to biking trails
- I&M Canal Access, Joliet (I&M Canal Trails)
- Black Road Access, Joliet (Rock Run Trail)
- Nichols Access, Joliet (Rock Run Trail)
- Hickory Creek Junction, Mokena (Old Plank Road Trail)

Special annual events sponsored by the Forest Preserve District of Will County

Island Rendezvous

Each second Saturday and Sunday in June, the Forest Preserve District of Will County hosts the Island Rendezvous at Isle a la Cache Museum, in Romeoville. This free, all-age family event is devoted the 18th-century fur trade between Native Americans and voyageurs, who came down from Canada via the continent's waterways to barter for beaver pelts with Native Americans. A voyageur encampment, canoe races, black-powder musket demonstration, and tomahawk throw are among the Rendezvous' features. Isle a la Cache Museum, devoted to this period of history, is open both days to provide a deeper understanding of the fur trade.

Fall Fest

To pay homage to the arrival of autumn and the traditional fall harvest, the Forest Preserve District of Will County holds an annual Fall Fest the fourth weekend in September. Hay rides, kids' activities, live music, and, of course, plenty of delicious food make for a perfect family outing—all against the colorful backdrop of Goodenow Grove Forest Preserve. The Saturday and Sunday program is free of charge, though food, crafts, and other items will be available for sale.

For more information call Forest Preserve District of Will County 815-727-8700.

Will County's Linear Trails

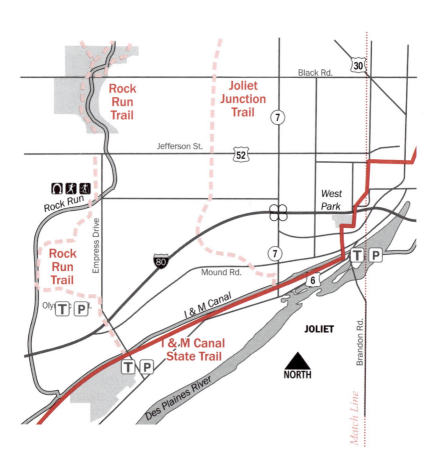

Walking in the Rock Run Preserve

Photo courtesy of Forest Preserve District of Will County

Old Plank Road Trail

Trail Length	21 miles
Surface	Asphalt, 10 feet wide
Information	Forest Preserve District of Will County 815-727-8700
Counties	Cook, Will

During the 1800s, early settlers in northern Illinois had the difficult task of moving wagons of grain and household good on dirt roads that connected rapidly growing communities and farms. With spring thaws and rains, the dirt roads became murky mire. One solution was to cover the dirt road with planks or wood laid side-by-side that provided a drier more stable surface. But by the 1880s the planks roads were largely replaced, sometimes by more efficient railway lines.

In the late 1970s, the Forest Preserve District of Will County and many other agencies, including Rich Township, the Illinois Department of Natural Resources, and the communities of Frankfort, Matteson, and Park Forest, formed the Old Plank Road Management Commission to preserve a 20 mile greenway on the right-of-way of an abandoned Penn Central rail line. The goal was to establish an east-west trail through wetlands, prairies, woodlands, and communities of Cook and Will Counties from Joliet east to Part Forest. After many years of planning and consensus building, a 13.1 mile section of the trail was open in the summer of 1997, running from Hickory Creek Junction Preserve, in Will County, east to Park Forest, in Cook County. The trail has been extended an additional

Old Plank Road Trail (continued)

7 miles west to Park Road, in Joliet Township, with the final mile to Washington Street being completed in 2006.

The Old Plank Road Trail is major link in the Grand Illinois Trail. Hickory Creek Junction, a half mile north of the trail, serves as an access point with parking and a pedestrian bridge over Highway 30. A half mile east of the trail's east trailhead is the Sauk Trail Woods and bicycle trail. The setting is urban with open and some wooded area.

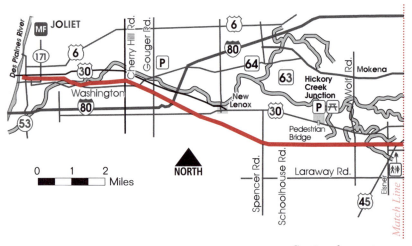

Continued on next page

Getting There   There are numerous opportunities to park and access the trail in the communities along the route. There is currently no designated parking at the eastern trailhead at Western Avenue. A good place to park is on the east side at Logan Park in Park Forest west of Orchard Drive and south of Route 30. Another good place to park is in

Frankfort. Take Route 45 south of Route 30 to White Street. Proceed south a half mile to Kansas Street. Parking is available to the right next to the village green, which is adjacent to the trail. To get to Hickory Creek Preserve, located in Mokena, take Route 30 (Lincoln Highway) west of Route 45 or east of Schoolhouse Road to the entrance.

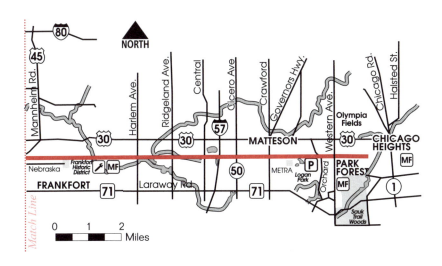

Wauponsee Glacial Trail

Trail Length	23.6 miles
Surface	Asphalt 3.3 miles, limestone screenings - remainder
Information	Forest Preserve District of Will County 815-727-8700
County	Will

The Wauponsee Trail is yet another regional trail of the Forest Preserve District of Will County built along an abandoned rail line. The Wauponsee Glacial Trail, named for an ancient lake that formed in Will County at the end of the last ice age, runs for 23.6 miles from Rowell Avenue, in Joliet, to the Kankakee River. Seventeen miles of the trail, from Joliet to the Village of Symerton, is scheduled for completion in 2006.

From Rowell Avenue to Sugar Creek Preserve on Laraway Road, the Wauponsee is surfaced with asphalt. The trail south of Laraway Road has a surface of limestone screenings, and is suitable for equestrian use. South of Manhattan, the trail runs along the eastern boundary of the Midewin National Tallgrass Prairie, and plans call for the Wauponsee to provide access to trails being developed within the Midewin by the U.S. Forestry Service. There are also plans to extend the Wauponsee to the Kankakee River State Park.

Getting There   Access to the Wauponsee Glacial Trail is located at Sugar Creek Preserve, .75 miles west of Route 52 in Joliet and at Manhattan Road Access located .25 miles west of Route 52 in Manhattan.

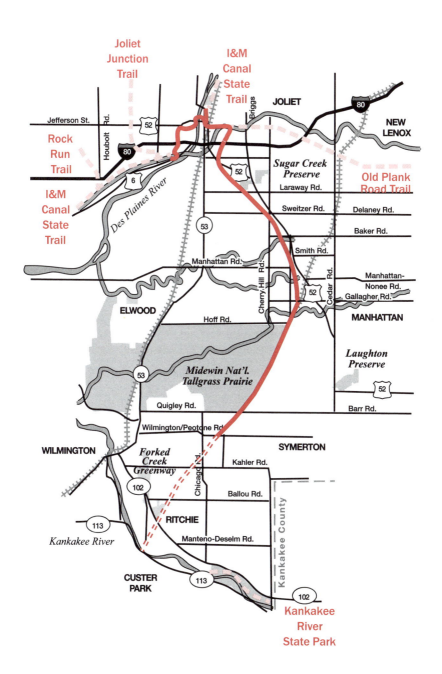

Rock Run Trail & the Joliet Trail Loop

Rock Run Trail

Trail Length	9 miles
Surface	Asphalt
Information	Forest Preserve District of Will County 815-727-8700
County	Will

Joliet Junction Trail Loop

Trail Length	4.4 miles
Surface	Asphalt
Information	Forest Preserve District of Will County 815-727-8700
County	Will

The Joliet Junction Trail, built along an abandoned rail line, parallels the Rock Run Trail and forms a 15 mile loop on the west side of the City of Joliet. This 4.4 mile, asphalt trail begins at Theodore Marsh Preserve, in Crest Hill and goes due south, paralleling Larkin Avenue, to where it intersects the I&M Canal State Trail. Using the I&M for a short distance takes you to the southern terminus of the Rock Run Trail, and doubling back on this trail to Theodore Marsh makes for a 15 mile outing.

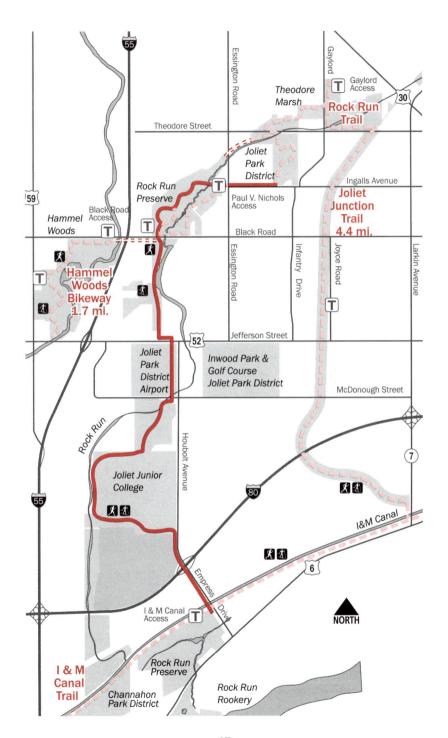

Rock Run Preserve
Black Road Access and Nichols Access

Connecting these two areas with the Rock Run Greenway are 2.5 miles of the Rock Run Trail. This paved trail takes visitors through prairie and around a small pond where many enjoy fishing. Picnicking is also popular at this preserve. Prairie and wetland projects at the preserve have improved plant and animal habitat. The Rock Run Trail connects the many forest preserves along the Rock Run waterway. For 9 miles, the trail follows the creek from Theodore Marsh in Crest Hill, to Nichols Access on Essington Road, to Black road Access, south to the Joliet Junior College, and ending at the I&M Canal Access on Houbolt (Empress Drive), in Joliet.

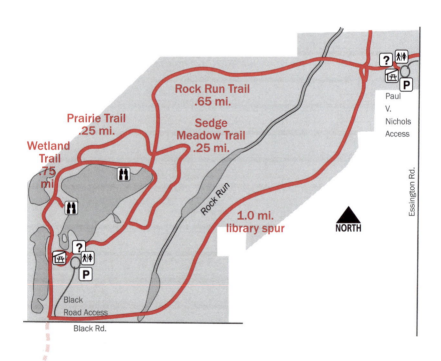

Rock Run Preserve
Theodore Marsh

Located in the heart of Crest Hill, Theodore Marsh is the trailhead to the Rock Run Trail and Joliet Junction Trail. The site provides a picnic area and a playground. Large wetland and prairie restoration projects are improving this site for wildlife. From this point, street routes connect cyclists to the I&M Canal State Trail on Route 6.

Getting There Rock Run Greenway – Theodore Marsh is located on Gaylord Road, approximately 0.25 mile north of Theodore Street, in Crest Hill.

Rock Run Greenway – Black Road Access is located on Black Road, approximately 0.25 mile east of the I-55 overpass, in Joliet.

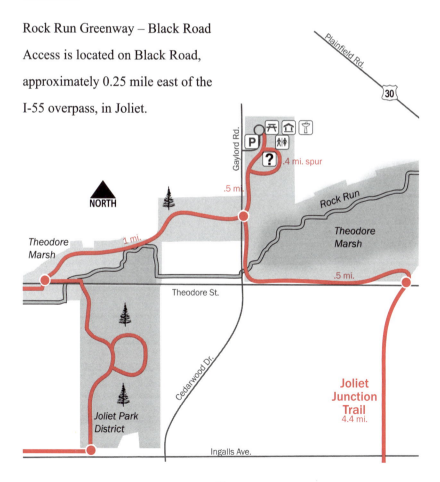

Will County I&M Canal Trail

Trail Length	11.4 miles
Surface	Asphalt, limestone screenings, packed earth
Information	Forest Preserve District of Will County 815-727-8700
County	Will

The Joliet I&M Canal Trail runs from Joliet to Romeoville for a total of 11.4 miles. The portion of the trail that begins at the Forest Preserve's Joliet Iron Works Historic Site is asphalt; the remainder of the trail to 135th Street is limestone screenings. The trail north of 135th Street to the Cook County line is crushed limestone/compacted earth.

From the Cook County line, the Centennial trail runs for a distance of 3.0 miles to Schneider's Passage. An old swing bridge from the Sanitary Shipping Canal was relocated along the trail just north of 135th Street.

At 135th Street is the Forest Preserve's District's Schneider's Passage, which provides a handful of parking spots for trail users. Just a short distance to the west of Schneider's Pass is the Forest Preserve's Isle a la Cache Museum, where plenty of additional parking is available. From 135th Street, in Romeoville, the trail goes south for a distance of 4.4 miles to Lockport. From Dellwood Park, in Lockport, the I&M Canal Trail continues to the Joliet Iron Works Historic Site for a distance of 3.3 miles. Limestone walls of the 19th century canal and ruins of the iron-making structures are featured along the way.

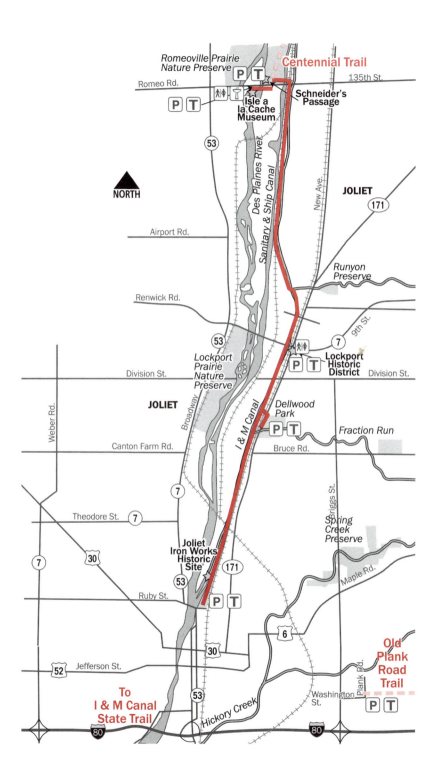

Centennial Trail (under development)

Trail Length	20 miles
Surface	Crushed stone
Information	Forest Preserve District of Will County
	815-727-8700
Counties	Will, Cook, DuPage

This planned 20 mile trail will run from the Chicago Portage site at Lyons in Cook County to Lockport in Will County. It forms a link in the Grand Illinois Trail. The setting is suburban with most services readily available.

For an interesting side hike, visit the Ottawa Trail Woods Preserve and the Chicago Portage Woods in Lyons. This is where Jolliet and Marquette discovered a connection between the Great Lakes and the Mississippi River. To get there take Harlem Avenue south of Joliet Road to the first entrance to the west for Ottawa Trail Woods Preserve. A little farther south on Harlem is the Chicago Portage Woods parking area. At Chicago Portage Woods is a National Historic Site honoring Marquette and Jolliet. A short footpath to the south takes you to portage Creek, and another to the west takes you to the Des Plaines River. In Ottawa Trail Woods, there is a footpath along the river leading to Laughton's Ford. Some two hundred years ago, Indian trails radiated out from this focal point.

From the portage site, the Centennial Trail will run on the north side of the Des Plaines River south to Willow Springs Road, then on a bridge crossing over the river. It then continues southwest between the river and the Chicago Sanitary & Ship Canal parallel to the Cook County I&M Canal Bicycle Trail. Southeast is the Palos Preserves. West of Palos, the

Centennial Trail enters DuPage County near the Waterfall Glen Forest Preserve, continuing southwest through Lemont and connecting to Lemont's canal trail.

In Will County, a 3 mile section of the Centennial Trail is open from the Cook/Will County line to 135th Street in Romeoville near the Isle a la Cache Museum.

Getting There   The northern trailhead will be located at the Chicago Portage National Historic Site in Lyons. Take Harlem Avenue south of Ogden Avenue and Joliet Avenue to 47th Street in Lyons. The entrance will be to the west. The southern trailhead is at Schneider's Passage on 135th Street, approximately 1.0 mile east of Route 53.

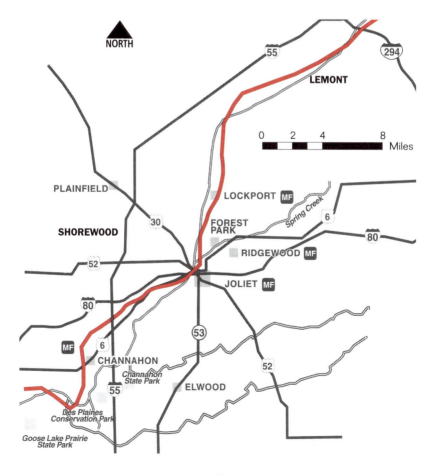

Photo courtesy of Michael Creagh, Forest Preserve District of Will County Volunteer

Northwestern Will County – Section 3

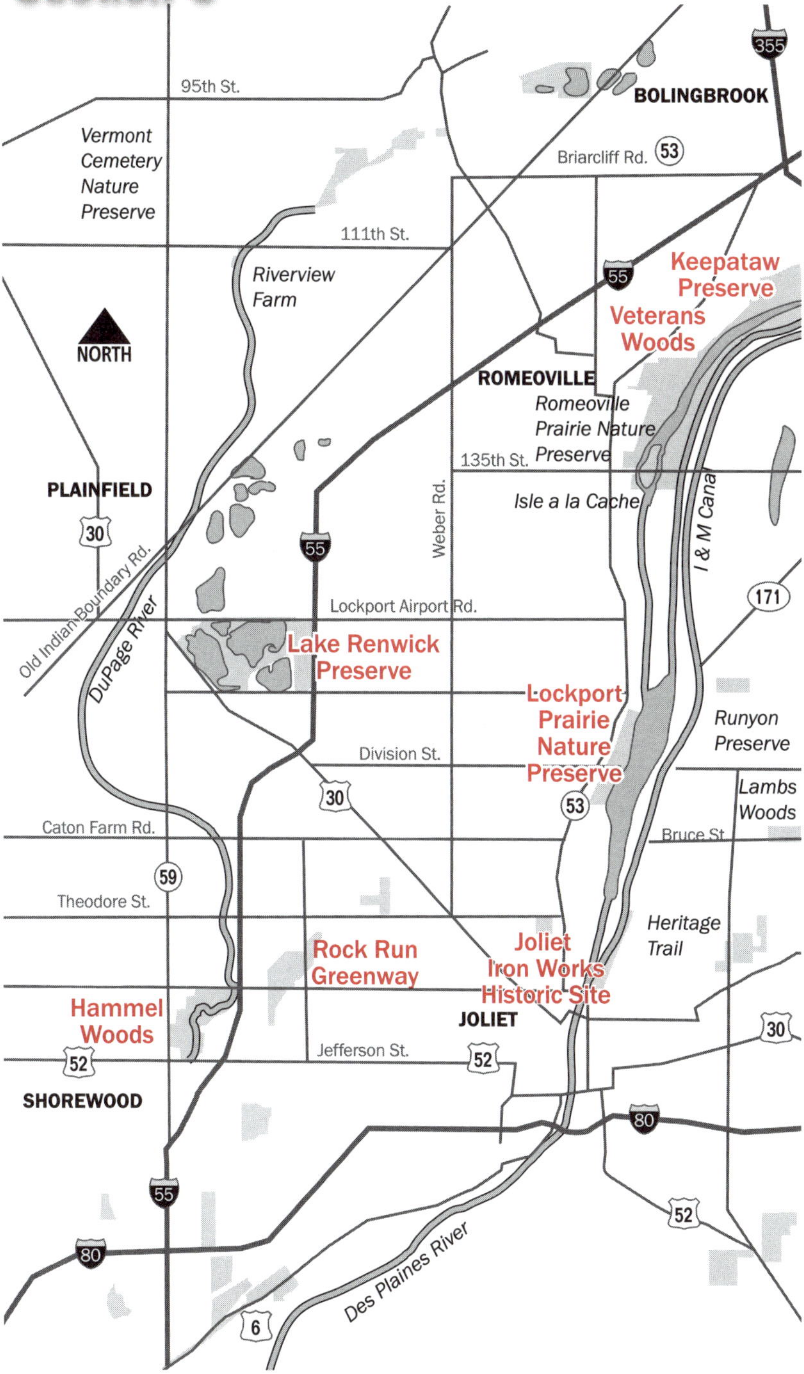

Gaylord Donnelley Canal Trail

Trail Length	2.5 miles
Surface	Asphalt, crushed limestone
Information	Lockport Township Park District 815-838-1183
County	Will

From downtown Lockport, the 2.5 mile Gaylord Donnelley Canal Trail extends north and south along the Will County I&M Canal, and connects to the I&M Canal State Trail system. A half mile south of the Public Landing are the massive limestone walls of I&M Canal Lock No.1. Five I&M Canal locks carried boats down the 40 foot drop from Lockport to Joliet.

The field headquarters for the construction of the National Heritage Corridor was located in Lockport. In downtown Lockport you will find the elegantly restored Gaylord Building, built with locally mined dolomite limestone. The building serves as an I&M Canal Visitor Center, and home to the Lockport Gallery of the Illinois State Museum.

Nearby are the I&M Canal Museum and a restored Pioneer Settlement. North of the Gaylord Building, the path heads north past the site of the original canal boat yard of the 1840's. The trail, tree-lined and well maintained, ends at 2nd Street. Here it connects to the Centennial Trail. South of Division for a mile and left of the I&M Canal is Dellwood Park. Here the trail is crushed limestone. If you are heading to Dellwood Park, walk your bike across the railroad tracks and past the narrow trail along the cliff. The wooden platform to the left leads along Fraction Run Creek to the Park.

Getting There From Route 53, take Route 7 (9th Street) across the high-level bridge and Canal Street. Just before the railroad trails, turn right into a city parking lot across from the Pioneer Settlement. From here you access the trail, which runs north and south along the bank of the old canal.

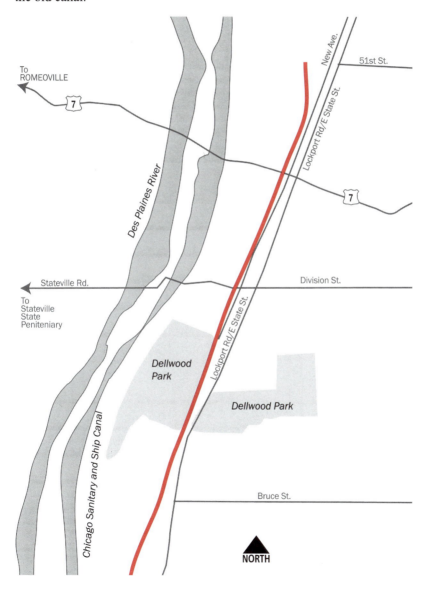

O'Hara Woods Nature Preserve

Trail Length	3 miles
Surface	Packed earth.
Contact	Romeoville Dept of Recreation 815-886-5573
County	Will

West of the canal is O'Hara Woods, a 70 acre natural prairie grove containing undisturbed mesic upland forest and savanna once typical of the area. It is one of the last undisturbed maple prairie groves remaining in northeastern Illinois. The 3 mile packed earth trail is unmarked. Near the entrance is a pavilion and picnic tables. During World War II the preserve was used to store dynamite. Twelve concrete foundations and several roads still remain.

Getting There   From Romeoville at the junction of Hwy 53 and Romeoville Road, take Romeoville Road west one mile, then north for .3 miles. The preserve is to the west.

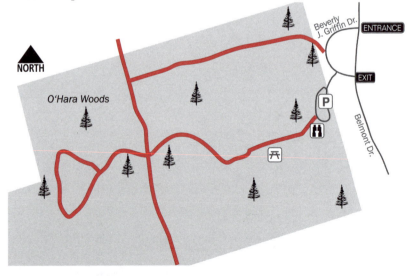

Keepataw Preserve

Trail Length	0.3 mile
Surface	Mowed turf
Information	Forest Preserve District of Will County 815-727-8700
County	Will

This short mowed turf trail loops through a new growth woodland on a 60 foot bluff overlooking the Des Plaines River. There is a scenic overlook of the river valley half way around the loop. There are no facilities at this site.

Getting There   Take Joliet Road north to Bluff Road and turn right (east). The entrance is on the south side of Bluff Road, 1 mile east of Joliet Road.

Veterans Woods

Trail Length	0.35 mile
Surface	Packed earth
Information	Forest Preserve District of Will County 815-727-8700
County	Will

Beautiful tall oaks are scattered throughout the grassy area near the shelter. Access to the trail is on the left across a bridge. The trail runs downhill into a large ravine. The site is popular with picnickers and there are shelters.

Getting There   Take Joliet for 1 mile south of I-55. There are two preserve entrances, Acorn Grove and Trader's Corners.

Lake Renwick Preserve – Turtle Lake Access/Lake Renwick Bikeway

Trail Length	2.9 miles
Surface	Paved
Information	Forest Preserve District of Will County 815-727-8700
County	Will

Opened in 2005, Turtle Lake Access is the trailhead to the 2.9 mile Lake Renwick Bikeway, an asphalt trail that runs through wetlands and lakes where egrets and herons forage. Turtle Lake Access also offers free, shoreline fishing on Turtle and Budde Lakes and day-use picnic areas.

Seasonal and site restrictions for fishing are required to protect the breeding and foraging habitat for the birds at Lake Renwick Heron Rookery Nature Preserve.

Getting There   Lake Renwick Preserve – Turtle Lake Access is located 1.0 mile east of Route 30 on Lockport Street, in Plainfield.

Lake Renwick – Heron Rookery Nature Preserve

Trail Length	1.5 miles
Surface	Packed earth
Information	Forest Preserve District of Will County 815-727-8700
County	Will

Lake Renwick was once a quarry for gravel mining operations, but now is a home for egrets and herons. There are 1.5 miles of hiking trails. From spring through August, great blue heron, black-crowned night-herons, cattle egrets, great egrets, and double-crested cormorants nest on two small islands in the middle of this 200 acre lake.

During the breeding season, March through August 15, the preserve is closed except for special bird viewing program. These programs are offered May 1 to August 15 every Wednesday at 10:00 am, and Saturday from 8:00 am to 12 pm. A forest preserve naturalist presents the program and sets-up spotting scopes for viewing. Be sure to check in at the visitor center. From August 16 through October, the preserve is open from 8:00 am to 8:00 pm and from November through February the preserve is open from 8:00 am to 5:00 pm.

Lake Renwick Heron Rookery is co-owned by the Illinois Dept. of Natural Resources and the Forest Preserve District of Will County.

Getting There   Lake Renwick Preserve – Lake Renwick Heron Rookery Nature Preserve is located on Renwick Road, 0.5 mile east of Route 30, in Plainfield. The Turtle Lake Access is located on Lockport Street, 1.0 mile east of Division Street, in Plainfield.

From Route 59 in Plainfield, take Route 30 (Plainfield Road) southeast to Renwick Road. Turn left (east) to the preserve entrance .5 miles east of Route 30 on the north side of the road.

Copley Nature Park is located on Route 30, 0.75 mile north of Renwick Road, in Plainfield.

Lake Renwick Preserve (continued)

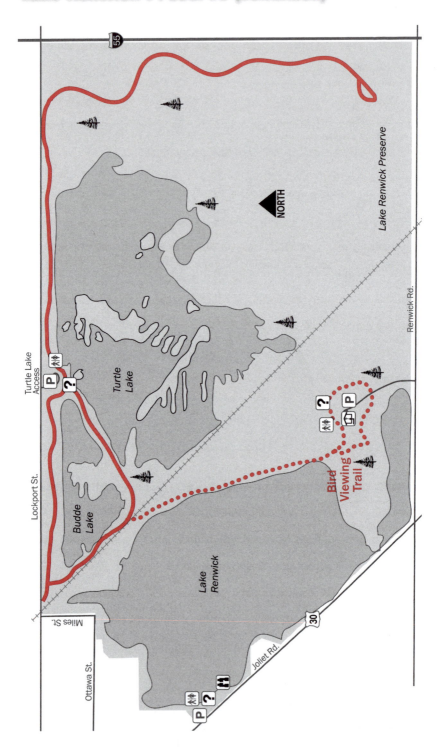

TRAIL LEGEND

▬▬▬	Trail-Biking/Multi
∙∙∙∙∙∙∙∙	Skiing only Trail
●●●●●●	Hiking only Trail
=========	Planned Trail
▬ ▬ ▬ ▬	Alternate Trail
▬▬▬	Road/Highway
++++++++	Railroad Tracks

AREA LEGEND

▢	City, Town
▢	Parks, Preserves
▢	Waterway
▢	Marsh/Wetland
▭▬▭	Mileage Scale
★	Points of Interest
– –	County/State
♣	Forest/Woods

Heron

83

Lockport Prairie Nature Preserve

Trail Length	0.4 mile
Surface	Packed earth
Information	Forest Preserve District of Will County 815-727-8700
County	Will

Thousands of years ago, the glaciers that once covered Lake Michigan melted. The draining water scoured the land down to the bedrock, forming the Des Plaines River Valley. Today, this area of exposed bedrock at Lockport Prairie is one of the best examples of dolomite prairie in Illinois.

Lockport Prairie's unique habitat is formed by water - cold, low in oxygen, and high in calcium-percolating through rocky bluffs and seeping out through the bottom. The preserve is notable for its high number of threatened and endangered species – both federal and state. Among the rare plants in the preserve is the Lakeside Daisy, which is found in only three other locations in the United States. The protected species now present are flourishing.

During your visit, look for the cool, clean rivulets unique to this type of habitat that flow through the prairie as you hike the 0.4 mile trail. Summer hours, between April and October, are 8:00 am to 8:00 pm. Winter hours, November through March, are 8:00 am to 5:00 pm.

Getting There Lockport Prairie Nature Preserve is located at Route 53 (Broadway) and Division Street, approximately 1 mile south of Route 7. Turn east on Division Street and follow to the trailhead.

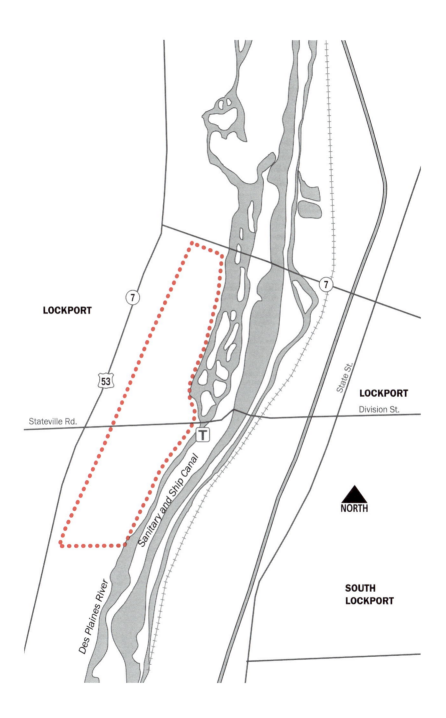

Joliet Iron Works Historic Site

In the 1850s, Joliet Iron Works began production of iron rails to meet the demands of the rapidly expanding railroad lines. The plant was located along the I&M Canal to provide waterway transportation for the incoming iron ore and for the outgoing finished iron rails.

In the first decade of the 20th century, the Joliet Iron Works was considered one of the most efficient steel producers in the country, employing close to 5,000 workers. During the depression of the 1930s demand for steel plummeted, and the Joliet Iron Works was shut down. The smoke stacks were removed and most of the large site has remained dormant. Today you can hike and bike through the site along the I&M Canal and near the Des Plaines River.

Getting There   Located in the southern section of Heritage Park. From the north take the Gaylord Donnelley Canal Trail through Lockport. From the south, take the I&M Canal State Trail to Brandon Road Lock and Dam and follow the National Heritage Corridor designated on-street bike route through Joliet.

Photo courtesy of Glenn P. Knoblock, Forest Preserve District of Will County

SYMBOL LEGEND	
🏊	Beach/Swimming
🚲	Bicycle Repair
🏠	Cabin
⛺	Camping
🛶	Canoe Launch
➕	First Aid
🍴	Food
GC	Golf Course
?	Information
🛏	Lodging
MF	Multi-Facilities
P	Parking
🎋	Picnic
👮	Ranger Station
🚻	Restrooms
🏠	Shelter
T	Trailhead
🏛	Visitor Center
🚰	Water
🔭	Overlook/Observation

Getting There
(continued)

By motor vehicle, take Route 53 into downtown Joliet. Take Route 53 (Scott Street) north of Route 30 to Columbia Street, then turn right where you will find a large parking area.

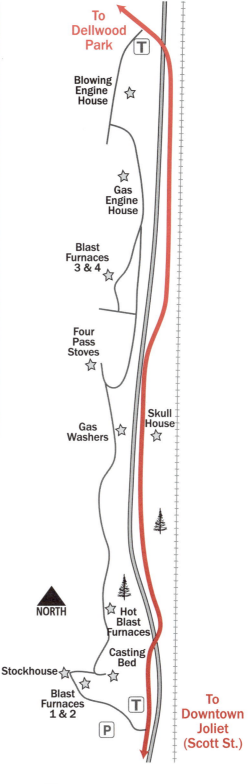

Pilcher Park

Trail Length	5 miles
Surface	Asphalt and gravel – 3 miles, woodchip – 2 miles
Information	Pitcher Park Nature Center 815-741-7277
County	Will

The 630 acre park is located in Joliet and includes Higinbotham Woods. There are 3 miles of multi-use path surfaced with asphalt and gravel, and 2 miles of hiking trails are surfaced with a mixture of woodchip and packed earth. The multi-use trails are mostly north of the Nature Center and can be accessed via an auto road or the gravel trail that loops around the nature center. This area of the park is quiet and serene. The asphalt trail was once an auto road now closed to auto traffic, and is in a deteriorating condition. A mountain or hybrid bike is recommended for both the asphalt and gravel paths.

There is a Nature Center and a large Horticultural Center. Programs are offered throughout the year. Drinking water and restrooms are available.

Getting There   Take Gougar Road north of Route 30. The entrance is .5 mile north of the intersection of Gougar and Route 30. Turn left into the parking area.

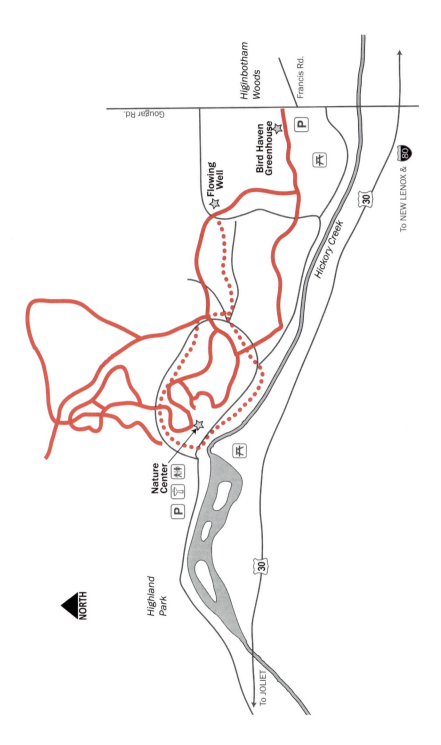

Hammel Woods
Hammel Woods Bikeway

Trail Length	3 miles
Surface	Paved, natural
Information	Forest Preserve District of Will County 815-727-8700
County	Will

Visitors to this 297 acre preserve can enjoy miles of trail that meander through mature forest and along a ridge overlooking the scenic DuPage River. This figure eight trail with a connecting spur is a great place for a quick aerobic workout. It's popular with the Joliet Bicycle Club because of the short but steep uphill and downhill at the bridged stream crossing. The trail is not technically challenging, but the eastern side of the northern loop does have some blind curves. The Crumby Recreation Area on Black Road offers the visitor a picnic pavilion, as does Hidden and Shorewood Shelters in the Route 59 Access area.

Getting There   Hammel Woods Hidden Shelter and Route 59 Access are located on Route 59, north of Route 52, in Shorewood.

Hammel Woods Crumby Recreation Area and DuPage River Access are located on Black Road, east of Route 59 in Shorewood.

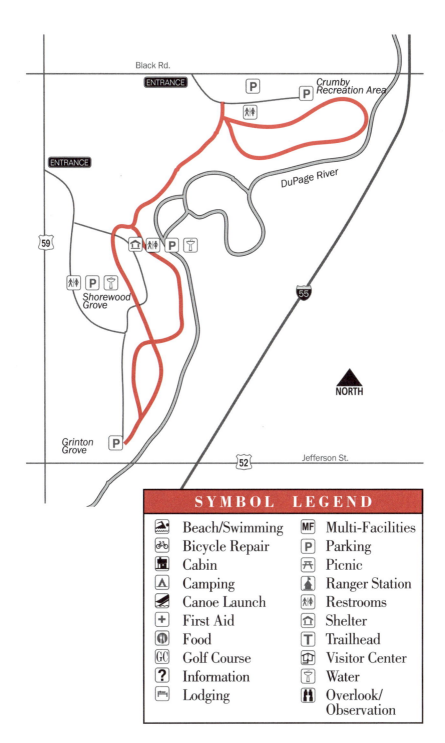

Sugar Creek Preserve

Information   Forest Preserve District of Will County
815-727-8700

County   Will

Located on the east side of Joliet, on Laraway Road near Route 52, Sugar Creek Preserve provides the main access to the Wauponsee Glacial Trail. The trail is named after an ancient glacial lake. Also located at Sugar Creek is the Forest Preserve's new visitor's center and Administration Center. Here visitors can obtain information on Forest Preserve trails, obtain permits, attend workshops and tours on natural gardening and building "green."

Orchard Orioles

Southwestern Will County — Section 4

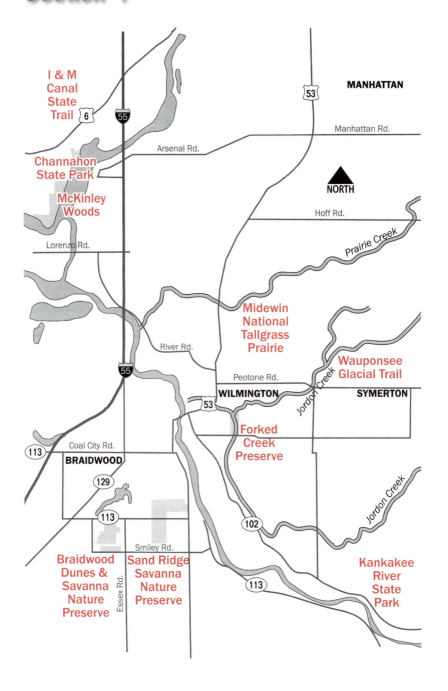

McKinley Woods

Trail Length	2.5 miles, access to the I&M Canal State Trail
Surface	Packed earth
Information	Forest Preserve District of Will County 815-727-8700
County	Will

This 473 acre preserve is located at a large bend in the Des Plaines River south of Channahon. As you enter McKinley Wood, the road leads through an upland forest and then down a steep hill into the river valley. McKinley Woods provides an excellent location to access the I&M Canal State Trail that runs through the preserve, and to overlook the ravines, canal, and the river. The entrance leads you downhill to the Boatsman Landing parking area. This is a good place to park for either the McKinley Woods trails or the nearby I&M Canal State Trail, which can be accessed a short distance to the south across the canal. Facilities include a nearby water pump, restrooms and shelters. Watch for occasional roots and stones on the trail. The beginning of the loop is at the intersection. The path right continues along the canal. As the trail turns north, it also starts a fairly steep climb. The return portion continues even farther up the hill.

Back at Boatsman Landing, access to the 1.2 mile Trail of the Old Oaks is west of the parking lot beyond a large mowed turf area. This trail has a steep climb with some scenic views of the canal and river. A spur to the left leads east to the River Bend Lookout parking area. The Trail of the Old Oaks continues to the right back down the valley to Boatsman

Landing. East of the Riverbend Lookout parking is the Upland Ski Trail consisting of two loops totaling .8 miles.

Getting There   McKinley Woods is located on McKinley Road, south of Route 6 and Bridge Road, in Channahon. From I-55, exit on Route 6 heading west. McKinley Road is 3.5 miles west of I-55. Head south on McKinley Road for 2 miles to the preserve entrance.

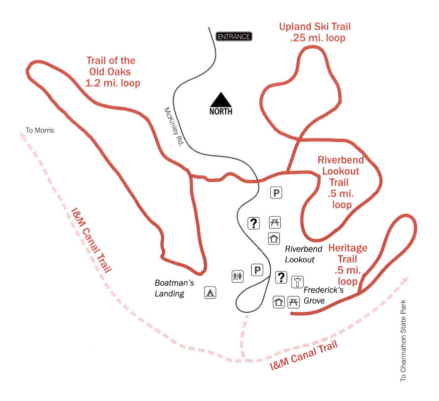

Braidwood Dunes & Savanna Nature Preserve

Trail Length	1.0 mile
Surface	Natural
Information	Forest Preserve District of Will County 815-727-8700
County	Will

The 325 acre Braidwood Dunes and Savanna offers a rare glimpse at the remains of an ancient sand dune created 11,000 years ago. It is one of the largest and most diverse examples of dry-mesic sand savannas in Illinois. At the dune ridges, you may discover the prickly pear cactus, which features yellow blooms atop its scratchy green cactus-like foliage in summer. As the path winds its way east out of the parking lot and into the black oak savanna, sandy sections of trail give way to impressions of hiking along the beach and trips to the wild west.

A 1 mile packed earth and land loop trail that is bisected by a cutback trail thereby forms a .5 mile loop. The trail gets muddy when wet. There is little shade for most of the hike. Also there are no facilities at Braidwood except for the parking lot and a port-a-toilet in summer. Box turtles, three-way sedges, six-line race runner lizards, prickly pear cacti, and tubercled orchids are just a few of the plant and animal species that can be found within the preserve. Picnickng, biking, and pets are not allowed as Braidwood is a dedicated state nature preserve.

Getting There   Braidwood Dunes and Savanna Nature Preserve is located on Route 113, east of Route 53 and I-55, approximately .75 mile east of Braidwood. Take I-55 south to Route 129. Head south on Route 129 to Route 113, then east. Turn right into the preserve parking lot.

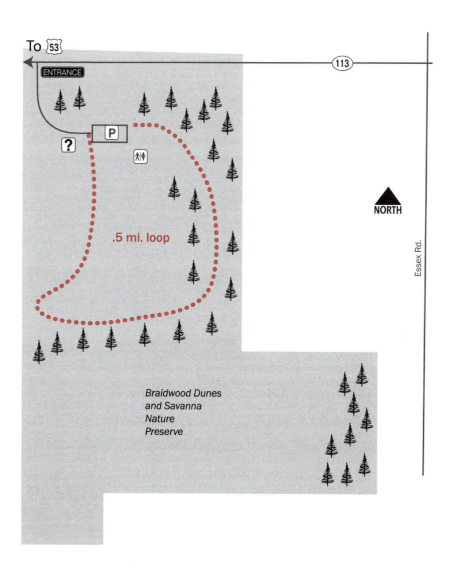

Forsythe Woods

Trail Length	2 miles
Surface	Natural
Information	Forest Preserve District of Will County 815-727-8700
County	Will

This 114 acre preserve is located south of the community of Wilmington. Jordan and Forked Creeks merge in the northwestern section of the preserve, and from there flows west 1.5 miles to join the Kankakee River. Head north past the shelter through the mowed turf area to access the woodland trails. Facilities include water, restrooms, a shelter and picnic tables, all near the parking area.

Getting There   Forsythe Woods is located on Kahler Road, 1 mile east of Route 102, in Wilmington. Take Route 53 to Route 102 near the Kankakee River in Wilmington. Take Route 102 southeast for .7 mile to Kalhler Road, then east to the preserve entrance on your left.

SYMBOL LEGEND

- Beach/Swimming
- Bicycle Repair
- Cabin
- Camping
- Canoe Launch
- First Aid
- Food
- Golf Course
- Information
- Lodging
- Multi-Facilities
- Parking
- Picnic
- Ranger Station
- Restrooms
- Shelter
- Trailhead
- Visitor Center
- Water
- Overlook/Observation

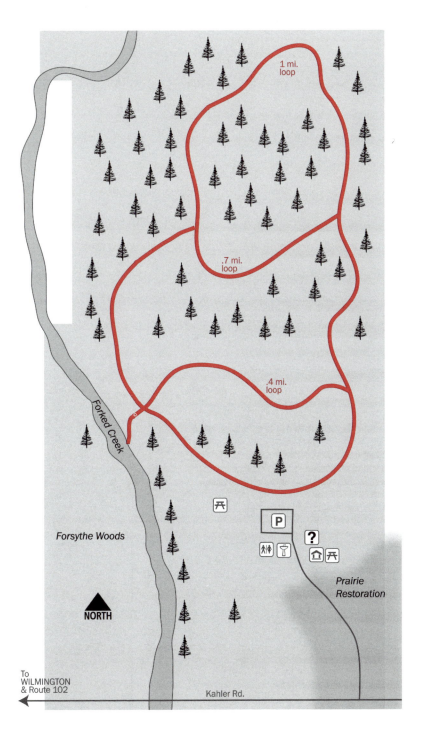

Channahon State Park

Information   Channahon State Park   815-467-4271
County   Will

Channahon State Park is the official trailhead for the Illinois & Michigan Canal State Trail, and is popular as a place from which to launch a canoe and paddling west toward Morris. Channahon is an Indian word meaning "the meeting of the waters" and signifies the joining of the DuPage, Des Plaines and Kankakee rivers. The Channahon Access became a state park in 1932. With the opening of the Illinois Waterway in 1933, the canal officially closed, after which it and its environs became extremely neglected and in desperate need of clean up and repairs. The Civilian Conservation Corps undertook this task, restoring Locks 6 & 7 in Channahon along with the locktender's house at Lock #6.

Photo courtesy of Joe Wittenkeller, Forest Preserve District of Will County Volunteer

An interpreter is on site four days a week to provide information and answer questions. Public programs and tours are available. Mature oak, walnut, ash and cottonwood trees provide a cool shaded setting for the visitor. Facilities include drinking water, pit toilets, picnic and playground areas, and primitive tent camping.

Getting There   From I-55, take the Route 6 Channahon exit. Turn west on Route 6 and continue into Channahon to Canal Street. Take a left on Canal and proceed to Story Street. Turn right on Story into the park and the parking area. There is addition parking at the Jessup Street parking area, one block further on Canal Street.

TRAIL LEGEND	
———	Trail-Biking/Multi
············	Skiing only Trail
••••••••	Hiking only Trail
=========	Planned Trail
− − − − −	Alternate Trail
▬▬▬▬	Road/Highway
+++++++++	Railroad Tracks

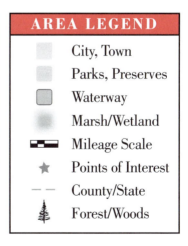

AREA LEGEND	
▪	City, Town
▪	Parks, Preserves
▪	Waterway
▪	Marsh/Wetland
▬▬	Mileage Scale
★	Points of Interest
− −	County/State
🌲	Forest/Woods

Midewin National Tallgrass Prairie

Trail Length	13 miles
Surface	Old roads
Information	Midewin National Tallgrass Prairie 815-423-6370
County	Will

Medewin National Tallgrass Prairie, consists of more than 19,500 acres, of which 6,370 acres are open to the public. A 1996 federal law established this site as the nation's first federally designated tallgrass prairie. The prairie includes grasslands, savanna, wetlands, seeps, upland forest, and several streams. There are some 23 miles of trail planned, of which 13 miles of temporary trails following routes on old roads of varying quality are now open. Quality varies and fat tire bicycles are recommended. There are over 10 miles of interim trail available from the Hoff Road Trailhead and parking lot. These are shared trails open to hikers, bicyclists, and equestrians.

From the Explosives Road Trailhead, you'll find two 1.5 mile hiking-only loops. There are no trails yet from parking lots identified as P1, P3, and P4 on River Road, eat of I-55. Picnic tables and portable toilet facilities are available at the Hoff Road and Explosives Road trailheads, and at the P3 parking lot. Water and flush toilets are available at the Midewin Welcome Center. Local wildlife abounds, especially grassland birds, white-tailed deer, turkeys, and coyotes. Midewin is home to 16 or more endangered and threatened species, including the loggerhead shrike. It also harbors Illinois' largest breeding population of upland sandpipers, a state endangered species.

Getting there Take I-55 south of Joliet to the Wilmington exit (#241). From this exit head east 4 miles to Route 53 (past the Wildlife Conservation Area). Turn left (north) on Route 53 for 1 mile to Midewin headquarters.

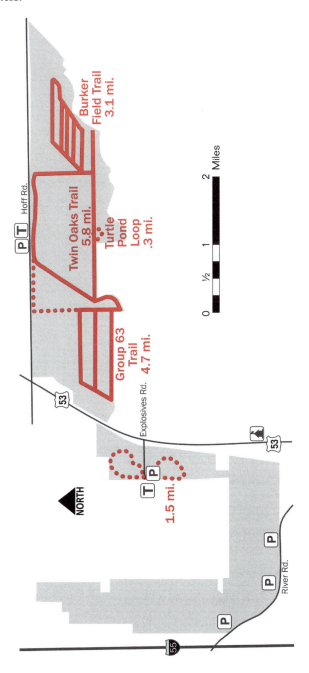

Kankakee River State Park

Trail Length	10.5 miles
Surface	Crushed limestone
Information	Kankakee River State Park 815-933-1383
County	Will

Kankakee River State Park offers you an unspoiled setting, open to hikers, bicyclists, canoeists, and other outdoor enthusiasts. The naturally channeled Kankakee River, listed on the Federal Clean Streams Register, is the focus of the park's popularity. It's approximately 4,000 acres envelope both sides of the Kankakee River for 11 miles. The park is within a region used by Illini and Miami Indians at the time of the first European contact in the 1670's. By the 1770s, the Potawatomi, Ottawa and Chippewa nations – "The Three Fires" – dominated the area. Following the Black Hawk Ware in 1832, the Potawatomi ceded all of their along the Kankakee and Illinois rivers to the United States. After the I&M Canal opened in 1848, the Kankakee and Iroquois Navigation Company established a waterway route on the Kankakee from the canal southwest of Channahon to Warner's Landing near present day Warner Bridge Road.

The bicycle/hiking trails begin at the Davis Creek area and travel to the Chippewa Campground. Effort level ranges from easy to moderately difficult. At one point the trail crosses a long suspension bridge. Watch out for washouts during the rainy season. Northwest of Rock Creek Canyon, the trail runs through woodlands with a steep downhill leading through an underpass of Warner Bridge Road before reaching the campground. Northwest of Route 102 and Dreselm Road is the 3 mile Chief Shaw-waw-nas-see Nature Trail, with views of limestone canyons and a frothy waterfall. South of the river are 12 miles of cross-country ski trails, and a 12 mile equestrian trail. Facilities in the park include a concession stand, camping, and picnicking areas. Canoe rentals are available at Bird Park in Kankakee (815-932-6555). It's a four to six hour trip to the park from there. Bicycle rentals are available at 815-932-3337. The Illinois Dept. of Natural Resources offers nature programs and guided hikes year-round.

Getting There   Both I-55 and I-57 provide convenient accesses. The main park entrance and Visitors Center is located off Route 103 just west of Deselm Road on the north side of the river.

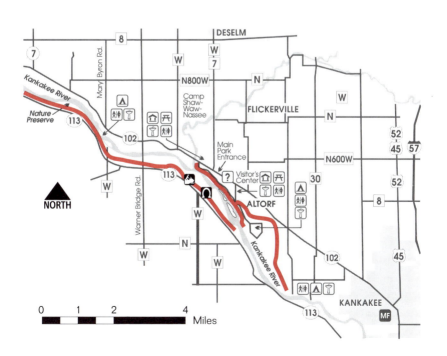

Central & Eastern Will County – Section 5

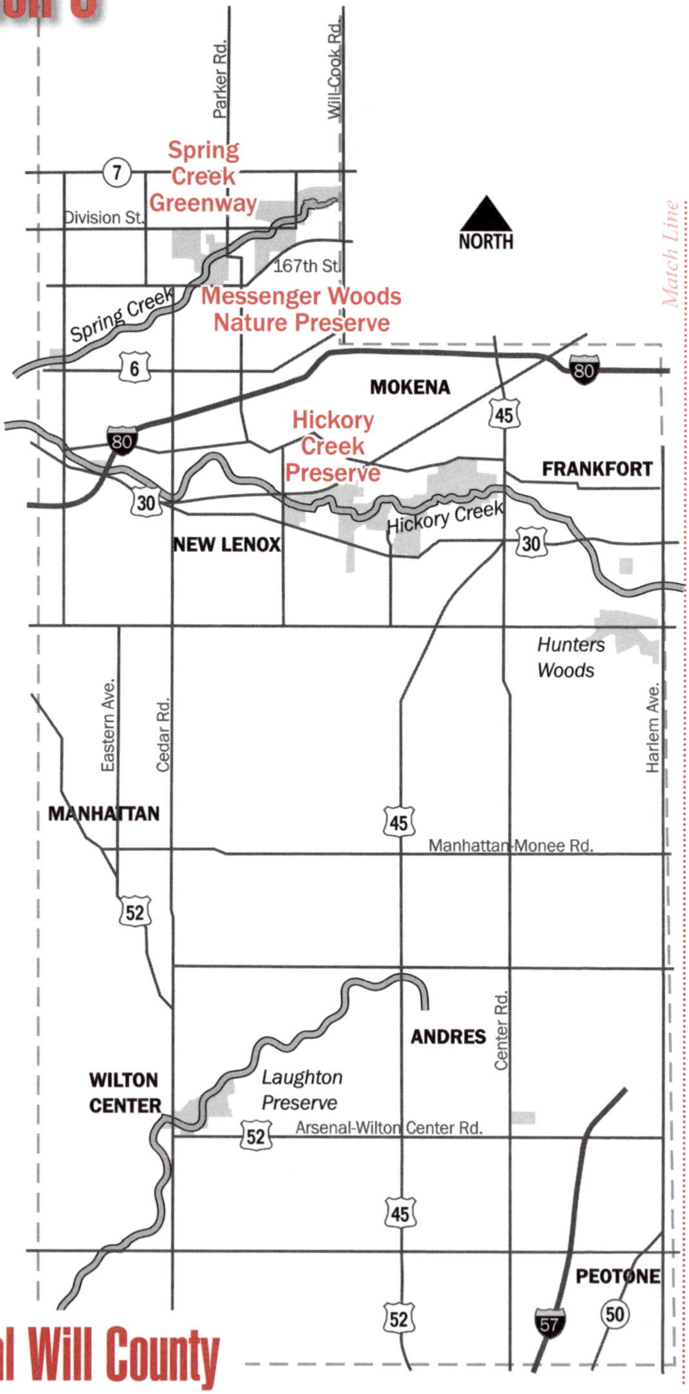

Parker Rd.
Will-Cook Rd.

Spring Creek Greenway

7

Division St.

167th St.

Spring Creek

Messenger Woods Nature Preserve

6

NORTH

Match Line

80

MOKENA

45

Hickory Creek Preserve

FRANKFORT

80

30

Hickory Creek

30

NEW LENOX

Hunters Woods

Eastern Ave.
Cedar Rd.
Harlem Ave.

MANHATTAN

45

Manhattan-Monee Rd.

52

ANDRES

Center Rd.

WILTON CENTER

Laughton Preserve

52

Arsenal-Wilton Center Rd.

45

52

PEOTONE

57

50

Central Will County

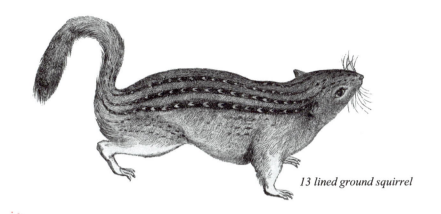

13 lined ground squirrel

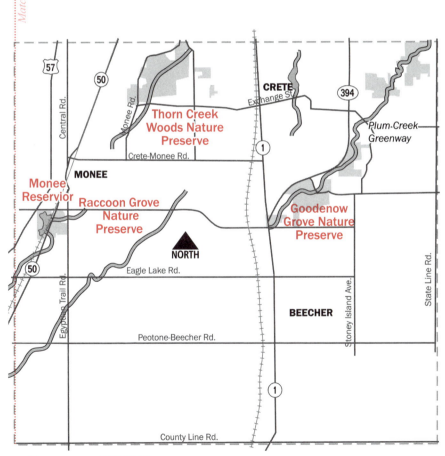

Eastern Will County

Spring Creek Preserve – Homer Trails

Trail Length	3.2 miles
Surface	Crushed limestone, mowed turf, packed earth
Information	Forest Preserve District of Will County 815-727-8700
County	Will

Homer Trails was established as an equestrian trail, but it is open to hikers and cross-country skiers. The trail consists of three loops with connector segments that tie the loops together. This is a 10 foot wide pathway that runs through open meadow, with parts running along a mature oak forest and overlook. The path is bumpy in spots from the horses' hoofs. The trail takes you past Spring Creek, which abounds with much wildlife including beaver, egrets, herons, muskrat, and fox.

Getting There   Spring Creek Preserve – Homer Trails' 154 acres are located on S. Bell Road, approximately ¼ mile south of 159th Street (Route 71), in Homer Township. Bell Road South is a short distance east of Bell Road-North on Route 7.

Central Will County

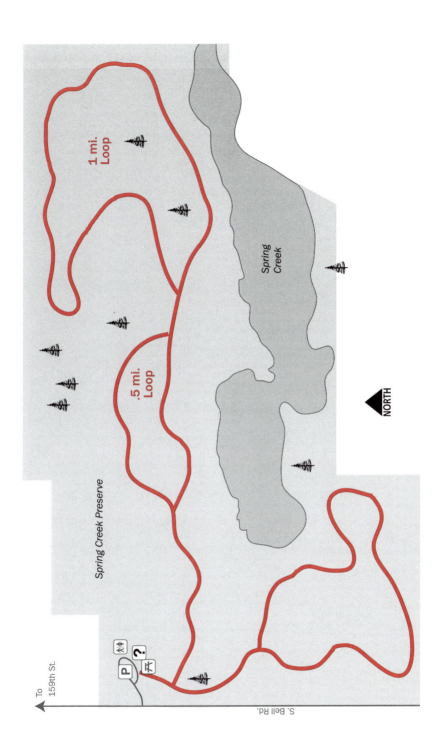

Messenger Woods

Trail Length	2 miles
Surface	Packed earth
Information	Forest Preserve District of Will County 815-727-8700
County	Will

This 947 acre preserve is located near Orland Park, and is on the Illinois Natural Area Inventory list because of its high-quality dry-mesic and mesic upland forest. It is noted for its beautiful spring wildflowers and rare nesting bird species. At least 146 native plant species have been recorded here. At the first shelter area, Oak Knoll, you can access a 1.5 mile loop trail. A short connector leads to the loop trail.

Taking the pathway south leads you through mature oak and maple forest, providing a quiet, serene spot with little traffic sounds. The relatively flat trail crosses the auto road and turns north. At the Hawthorn Shelter area, you will come to a clearing and the trailhead for a .5 mile nature trail. To hike the nature trail, cross the stone bridge over Spring Creek and head north along a ridge overlooking a ravine. Here the terrain is a bit more hilly. In spring, the forest floor is filled with white trillium, bloodroot, blue-eyed Mary, and Virginia bluebells. Facilities include drinking water, restrooms, picnic tables and shelters at both the Hawthorn and Oak Knoll areas.

Central Will County

Getting There Messenger Woods is located on Bruce Road, north of Route 6 (Southwest Highway) and east of Cedar Road, in rural Lockport. Take Cedar Road north of Route 6 or south of Route 7 to Bruce Road. Head east on Bruce staying left at the Y. The preserve entrance is to the north.

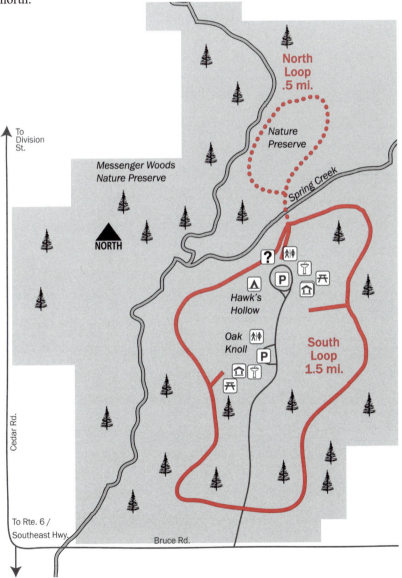

Hickory Creek Preserve/Bikeway
East Branch and West Branch

Trail Length	2.8 miles paved & 1 mile earth – West Branch
	1.8 miles – East Branch
Surface	Asphalt and packed earth
Information	Forest Preserve District of Will County
	815-727-8700
County	Will

Hickory Creek Preserve, located south of Mokena and north of Frankfort, is the largest site in the Forest Preserve District of Will County. The stream that bears its name runs through the preserve on its way west to the Des Plaines River. The preserve is divided into two sections separated by Wolf Road. The eastern section includes a 1.8 mile asphalt trail as well as two short packed earth hiking-only trails that loop off the main trail. The hiking trails total .9 miles.

The trail heads south from the La Porte Road parking area. The pathway leads downhill through an open meadow. A long bridge crosses over Hickory Creek as you enter a forest. Tall oak trees line the path. The trail is relatively hilly and features a couple of good climbs along the way. The path ends at the Frankfort Township Swimming Pool at Route 30 where parking is also available. The Hickory Hollow Shelter north of the trailhead parking area also avails restrooms and a water pump.

The west section includes a 2.8 mile trail that connects the Forest Preserve's Hickory Creek Barrens, on Schoolhouse Road, in New Lenox to Hickory Creek Junction, in Mokena. This 10 foot wide trail is asphalt

Central Will County

and passes through prairie and dense woodlands and crosses Hickory Creek. Parking is available at both Hickory Creek Junction and, on the western end of the trail, at the Hickory Creek Barrens Access on School House road. Here is located the Schmuhl School, a 19th century, one room schoolhouse owned by the New Lenox Historical Society. West of Wolf Road, at Hickory Creek Junction, you will find access to the Old Plank Road Trail, as well as the trailhead to the Hickory Creek Bikeway – West Branch.

Getting There   Hickory Creek Junction is located on Route 30, 1 mile west of Wolf Road, in Mokena. Hickory Creek Barrens Access is located on Schoolhouse Road, .25 mile north of Route 30, in New Lenox.

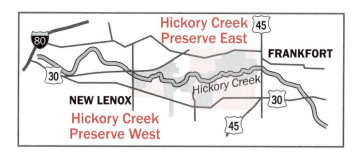

SYMBOL	LEGEND
Beach/Swimming	Multi-Facilities
Bicycle Repair	Parking
Cabin	Picnic
Camping	Ranger Station
Canoe Launch	Restrooms
First Aid	Shelter
Food	Trailhead
Golf Course	Visitor Center
Information	Water
Lodging	Overlook/Observation

Hickory Creek Preserve/Bikeway West Branch

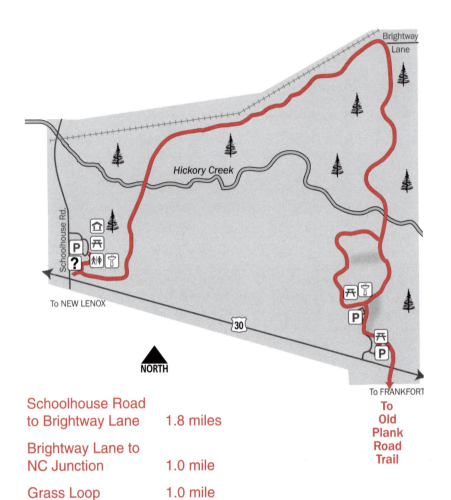

Schoolhouse Road to Brightway Lane	1.8 miles
Brightway Lane to NC Junction	1.0 mile
Grass Loop	1.0 mile

TRAIL LEGEND

———	Trail-Biking/Multi
··········	Skiing only Trail
••••••••	Hiking only Trail
= = = = =	Planned Trail
- - - - -	Alternate Trail
———	Road/Highway
+++++++	Railroad Tracks

Central Will County

Hickory Creek Preserve/Bikeway East Branch

Monee Reservoir

Trail Length	2.5 miles	
Surface	Mowed turf	
Information	Monee Reservoir	708-534-8499
County	Will	

The 146 acre Monee Reservoir was built to help control flooding and provide a water recreation area for fishing and boating. The adjoining wetlands attract waterfowl and other animals. East of the parking area near the boat dock, there is access to 2 miles of mowed turf hiking trail through a wetland north of the lake. North of the wetland area is a .5 mile loop trail through a meadow. There is also a short asphalt-walking path running along the lake by the boat dock. There is a year-round concession/visitor center where you can rent rowboats, pedal boats, and canoes.

The visitor center is open from 6 am to 7 pm from April thru October and from 8 am to 4 pm from November thru March. Drinking water and restrooms are available. Picnic tables and shelters can be found at Bluegill Hill, Catfish Corner, and Monee Grove. The Monee Reservoir is separated from Raccoon Grove Nature Preserve by the Illinois Central Gulf railroad tracks and Route 50.

Getting There   Take governors Highway (Route 50) 2 miles south of Monee or north of Peotone to Pauling Road. Head west on Pauling .7 mile to Ridgeland Avenue. Turn left on Ridgeland and proceed south .3 mile to the entrance on the left. Park in the lot near the concession/visitor center.

Eastern Will County

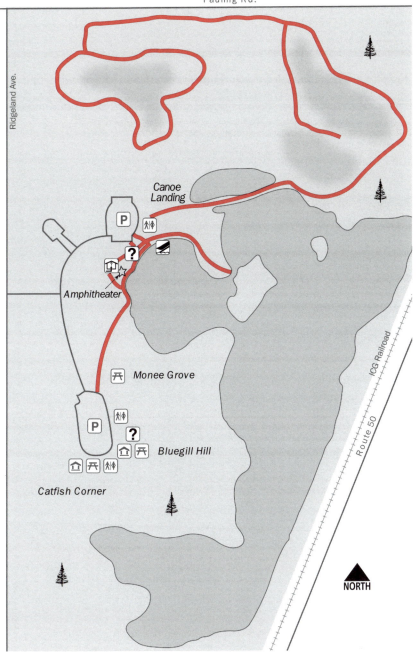

Raccoon Grove Forest Preserve

Trail Length	0.5 mile
Surface	Natural
Information	Forest Preserve District of Will County 815-727-8700
County	Will

Raccoon Grove is 202 acres of upland and floodplain forest, savanna and stream habitats. In the mesic upland forest, basswood, sugar maple, and an occasional white ash dominate. In contrast, the southern portion of the property was savanna, prairie, and open oak woodland prior to settlement, and is being restored. The preserve is situated on the front slope of the West Chicago Moraine, the terminal moraine of the Valparaiso Moraine System which was deposited during the late Ice Age upon retreat of the glaciers 15,000 years ago.

The .5 mile trail leads visitors through gently rolling hills and down into the mesic floodplain, where one can find Virginia waterleaf, bladdernut and even a few pawpaw. As the trail begins to loop back into the dry-mesic upland forest, it follows along and above Rock Creek. In the spring, visitors can enjoy woodland violets, yellow and white trout lilies, Dutchman's Breeches, and red trillium.

Getting There   From I-57 exit 335 going south. Turn right onto Manhattan-Monee Road. After a short distance turn left onto Ridgeland Avenue. In about two miles it ends in a T. Turn left onto Pauling Road, which passes over the interstate. Within a mile, the road will bridge over railroad tracks. The entrance to Raccoon Grove is the next right.

Eastern Will County

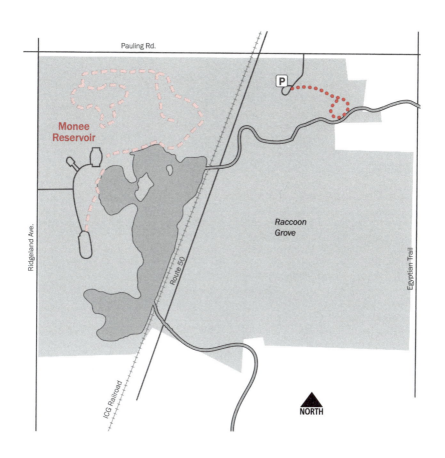

SYMBOL LEGEND

- 🏊 Beach/Swimming
- 🚲 Bicycle Repair
- 🏠 Cabin
- ⛺ Camping
- 🛶 Canoe Launch
- ➕ First Aid
- 🍴 Food
- GC Golf Course
- ❓ Information
- 🛏 Lodging
- MF Multi-Facilities
- P Parking
- 🍽 Picnic
- 🏛 Ranger Station
- 🚻 Restrooms
- ⛺ Shelter
- T Trailhead
- 🏛 Visitor Center
- 🚰 Water
- 🔭 Overlook/Observation

Thorn Creek Woods Nature Preserve

Trail Length	2.5 miles
Surface	Packed earth
Information	Thorn Creek Nature Center 708-747-6320
County	Will

Thorn Creek Woods is located near the Cook County line in Park Forest. Its 850 acres consist of woodlands, prairie, and wetlands. The dry mesic oak hickory forest is dominated by 150 year old white and red oak trees with a rich understory of native shrubs and spring wildflowers. The diverse terrain also includes Thorn Creek and its tributaries, glacial pothole ponds and marshes, successional old fields and prairie remnants. The woods provide an excellent spot for a quiet walk on the 2.5 miles of packed earth hiking trails that meander through the preserve.

The half mile Nature Center Loop winds through second growth woods. The 1.25 mile Woodland Trail crosses Thorn Creek and wanders through bottomlands, ravines and upland woods. The three quarter mile Owl Lake Trail continues to the glacial pothole at the southwestern portion of the preserve. Seasonal trail guides are available in the Nature Center and at the information kiosk at the trailhead.

Getting There   Thorn Creek Nature Center is located on the east side of Monee road just north of Stuenkel Road in Park Forest.

Eastern Will County

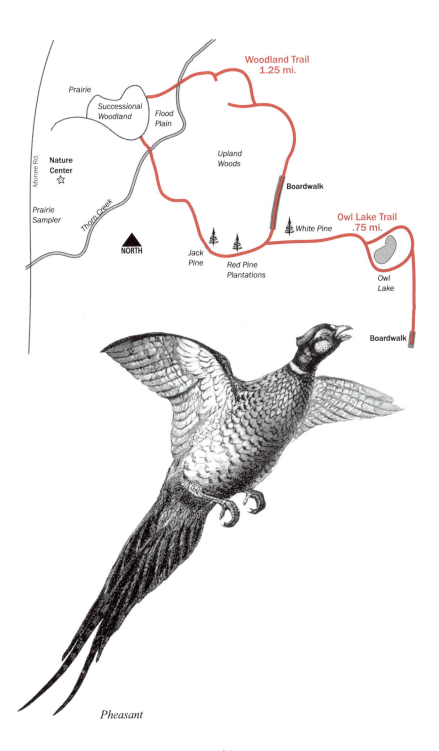
Pheasant

Goodenow Grove Nature Preserve

Trail Length	3.5 miles
Surface	Paved, gravel, natural
Information	Forest Preserve District of Will County 815-727-8700
County	Will

This is Will County's eastern-most preserve. It is located south of Crete and less than 5 miles from Indiana. There are 3.5 miles of hiking trails surrounding Plum Creek Nature Center. At the nature center, named for the creek that flows through the preserve, you will find environmental exhibits and displays. A 1 mile gravel loop trail starts west of the nature center and heads north through Thorn Apple Meadow, then loops back to the nature center. A 1 mile packed earth hiking trail heads east off of the gravel trail through a woodland. There are also three shorter loop trails of .3 to .5 mile to the north, west, and south of the center, and a .3 mile interpretive trail, the Trail of Thoughts, starting at the Nodding Oaks picnic area near the nature center.

For a view of the surrounding countryside, climb the sledding hill in the middle of the preserve. Restrooms, drinking water, and a public phone are available at the nature center, which is open Tuesday to Saturday from 10:00 am to 4:00 pm and Sunday from noon to 4:00 pm.

Getting There   Goodenow Grove is located 1.25 miles east of the intersection of Routes 1 and 394 on Goodenow Road, south of Crete.

Eastern Will County

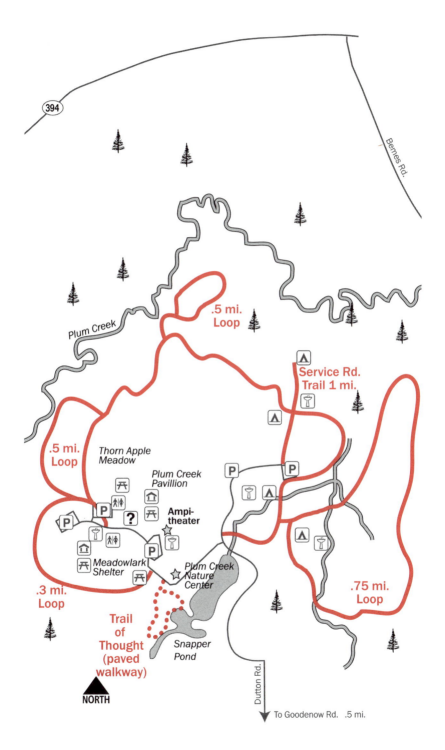

The Illinois & Michigan Canal State Trail and nearby parks — Section 6

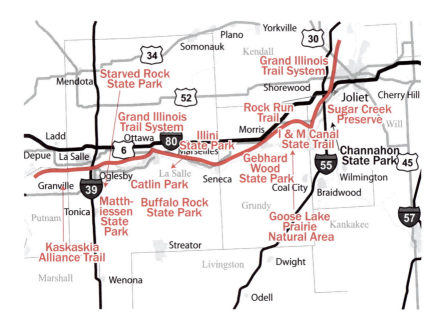

A Great Egret Nest

Photo courtesy of Forest Preserve District of Will County

The Illinois and Michigan Canal State Trail

Trail Length	61.5 miles
Surface	Limestone screenings
Information	I&M Canal State Trail Headquarters
	815-588-6040
Counties	Will, Grundy, LaSalle

This 61 mile multi-use biking and hiking state trail is the backbone of the I&M Canal National Heritage Corridor trail system. It runs along the south side of the canal from Brandon Road Lock and Dam southwest of Joliet to LaSalle/Peru at Route 351. When the canal was in active use, the trail served as the towpath for the drivers who guided horses and mules along the canal embankment. They pulled barges laden with grain and corn to the East Coast, and westbound barges of finished goods and products manufactured in the East for use by the farmers and settlers in the rapidly growing Midwest.

Along the way you will pass through the communities of Channahon, Morris, Seneca, Marseilles, Ottawa, Utica, and LaSalle. The Channahon, W.G. Stratton, Gebhard Woods, and Buffalo Rock State Parks as well as the Will County McKinley Woods Forest Preserve and Rock Run Preserve offer easy access to the state trail. Nearby are numerous other inviting natural areas, such as Starved Rock and Matthiessen State Parks and the 19,500 acre Midewin National Tallgrass Prairie.

The trail is owned and maintained by the Illinois Dept. of Natural Resources. (DNR). It is relatively straight and flat, and is well maintained, but you may experience occasional washouts. Food, drink and restrooms can be found in the several communities, parks, and forest preserves adjacent to the trail. However we suggest you bring along water and snacks, as there are quite a few miles between some of them. The DNR has provided several camping sites along the trail.

Photo courtesy of Ron Panzer, Forest Preserve District of Will County Volunteer

We'll start our 61 mile tour along the trail by starting at Brandon Road Lock and Dam, the eastern trailhead, and ending by the canal boat basin in LaSalle. The trailhead is north of Route 6 off Brandon Road on the outskirts of Joliet. A massive lock and dam system operates south of Route 6 (Channahon Road) as part of the Illinois Waterway System. You can see the lock by driving south of Route 6 to the Visitors Center, and perhaps observe the system in operation transporting a passing barge.

The Illinois and Michigan Canal State Trail (continued)

The trail runs south of and near the I&M Canal which becomes a separate waterway again near Brandon Loc. In Joliet, the canal shares a common channel with the Des Plaines River. The trail runs north of Route 6 and the river. Across the Des Plaines river is the Midewin National Tallgrass Prairie. An underpass at Bush Road is the only road crossing over the 5.5 mile section to I-55. The trail passes by gravel mining operations with tall hills of sand and gravel left by the last glacier. The Will County Rock Run Preserve provides the only I&M Canal access between Brandon Road and Channahon. Rock Run Preserve is approximately 3.5 miles from the eastern trailhead at Brandon Road. Parking, water, restrooms and picnic areas are available at the preserve.

At 5.5 miles out from Brandon Road you will pass under I-55. Farmland gives way to a forest south of the trail. Near Channahon an underpass comes into view. Be careful of the limited clearance. The path runs along a residential area with a road crossing at Knapp Street before entering Channahon State Park at 9.5 miles out. At the park you'll find parking, water, shelters, picnic tables, restrooms, and campsites available. While here visit the original locktender's house, Lock #6 on the east side and Lock #7 on the west side of the spillway.

South of Channahon, occasional stone overlooks near Moose Island provide scenic vistas along the waterway. Across the river, a marina, homes, and a water filtration plant line the bank. Farther south, woodland separates the trail from the river. At 12.5 miles out, a big bend in the canal and the river, you will come to the entrance to McKinley Woods, a Will County forest preserve. Take the bridge across the canal at Boatsman Landing. This beautiful preserve has excellent hiking trails as well as water, restrooms, picnic tables, shelters, and camping facilities. This is also a convenient place to park for a day trip or overnight. The entrance to the park is at the end of McKinley Woods Road. West of McKinley Woods the Des Plaines River converges with the Kankakee River, which flows northeast from Kankakee County, to form the Illinois River.

Continuing on you will soon see the large Dresden Nuclear Power Plant across the river, in operation since 1960. At 15.5 miles out is the Dresden Island Lock & Dam. To see the lock and dam, take the short path to the left. Parking is available here. Across the canal are the remains of the small village of Dresden. West of Dresden Island the path is shady with woodlands lining the trail. After two underpasses and a road crossing at South Taber Road, you will come to the Aux Sable Aqueduct at 17.5 miles out. Here the Aux Sable Creek, on its way to the Illinois River, crosses the canal. You will also find Lock #8 and an old locktender's residence west of a aqueduct. A one-room schoolhouse, a boarding house, blacksmith, sawmill and a distillery were once in operation here as well. Two miles south of the canal, across the river, are Goose Lake Prairie State Natural Area and Heidecke Lake.

The Illinois and Michigan Canal State Trail (continued)

West of Aux Sable, the trail leads through a wetland and then dense woodland. Cemetery Road parallels the trail from Dresden to Morris. Residences line the canal to the north as you enter the community of Morris. The wide Illinois River rejoins the canal trail here. William G. Stratton State Park is nearby, where you will find parking, restrooms and drinking water. The trail passes under busy Route 47, and then a much smaller iron trail bridge that crosses the canal and leads to Canal Point Plaza in downtown Morris.

Continuing west you will soon come to an old stone aqueduct over Nettle Creek at Gebhard Woods State Park. West of the aqueduct is the trail bridge that takes you across the canal into the state park. Take a pause and walk through the picturesque park and long Nettle Creek to enjoy an abundance of wildlife. Gebhard is a good spot if you want to leave your vehicle overnight. Parking, a camping area, drinking water, restrooms, and picnic areas are available. Also at Gebhard you will find the .8 mile Nettle Creek Nature Trail. This is a hiking-only packed earth-surfaced pathway that winds through stately oak trees and along the creek. There is a crushed limestone trail that runs for a short distance along the north side of the canal east to Nettle Creek and the aqueduct.

Continuing west of Morris, Old State Road parallels the trail and canal to the north. The setting here is cornfields, woodlands, and wetlands, with an occasional residence. Along the way, you'll pass through picturesque tunnels of trees in many spots.

The trail crosses Main Street in Seneca at 34.5 miles out. Restaurants are nearby and there is a shelter with picnic tables to provide a good spot for a break. West of Seneca Route 6 parallels the trail to the north

clarkia pulchella

into Marseilles. You will encounter a few curves and small hills on the trail path between Seneca and Ottawa. As you approach Marseilles, you will pass Locks #9 and #10. The trail leads through two underpasses including one under Main Street. For an interesting side trip, take the pedestrian crossing on the Main Street bridge south across the rapids to the Illinois River to Illini State Park. The Mareseilles Lock and Dam is west of the park.

Heading west from Marseilles, the trail leads through another woodland. Be aware of the numerous caution signs here with several curvy sections,

The Illinois and Michigan Canal State Trail (continued)

small bridge crossings, and loose gravel. At 46.5 miles out, you will come to the Fox River Aqueduct. The river is the last of the Chicagoland rivers to join the Illinois on its journey to the Mississippi.

Following a road crossing and two underpasses, the trail enters a residential neighborhood on the east side of Ottawa. South of the trail in downtown Ottawa on Route 23 is the Reddick Mansion, where the first Lincoln-Douglas debate was held. W. D. Boyce, the founder of the Boy Scouts of America lived in Ottawa. In the early 1900s, Ottawa was the leading glass producer in the world because of the ideal sand found in the area. West of Ottawa you will pass Lock #11 and #12. The limestone cliffs north of the trail are noticeable a good part of the rest of the way to LaSalle.

duck

Across the road at 51 miles out is the access to Buffalo Rock State Park and the Effigy Tumuli. Along Dee Bennett Road is a large, paved parking area for trail users. Southwest of Buffalo Rock is Blue Lake. The water is a beautiful turquoise color due to the sale deposits from the nearby silica mines. There are camping sites nearby. West of Blue Lake is a large wetland on both sides of the trail. This is where the canal loses its contained linear nature and becomes part of the extensive wetland. Approaching Utica, the trail widens and has an asphalt surface. You enter the community of Utica at 56.5 miles out. Proceed up the small hill at the Utica Elevator Company. Take the pedestrian bridge across the canal. The LaSalle County Historical Society Museum is on Route 178 north of the trail. Starved Rock and Mathiessen State Parks are south of there. West of Utica, the CSXT railroad tracks parallel the trail and canal to the north, and you'll come to limestone cliffs on both sides of the trail. Approaching LaSalle is Split Rock Lake.

Continuing west are tow huge bridges that cross the canal and the Illinois River. The first is for Routes 39 and 51. One last aqueduct west of the bridge crosses Little Vermilion Creek. Then you come to the bridge for Route 351. The western trailhead is near Lock #14 at 61 miles out. Restrooms, picnic tables and parking are nearby. The stairs lead to downtown LaSalle. Peru is to the west.

To get to the western trailhead in LaSalle, take 351 south of I-80 at the LaSalle exit. Turn right on Route 6 and head west to Joliet Street. Go south on Joliet Street for 5 blocks to Canal Street. The parking area entrance is a short distance to the west.

The Illinois and Michigan Canal State Trail (continued)

One of the largest earth sculptures ever built, the Effigy Tumuli is located near the park. This reclaimed mine site has turned a barren wasteland into an area filled with recreational opportunities and interesting landscapes. It contains five large earthen figures (effigies) of native aquatic animals. Represented in geometric forms are a water strider, frog, catfish, turtle and a snake.

BUFFALO ROCK STATE PARK

Directions: Boyce Memorial Drive south to Ottawa Avenue. West 1.8 miles, past Naplate, to the park entrance. Located five miles from the Fox River Aqueduct on the north bank of the Illinois River. Atop the sandstone bluff at the summit of Buffalo Rock is a sweeping view of the Illinois River. It has several picnic areas.

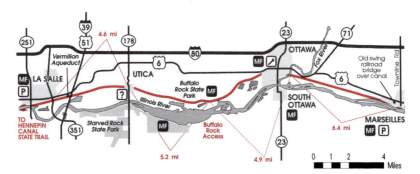

LA SALLE
Parking off Canal St. one half block south of Joliet St.

OTTAWA
Sight of the first Lincoln-Douglas Debate, Reddick Mansion, Fox River Aqueduct and other historic attractions.

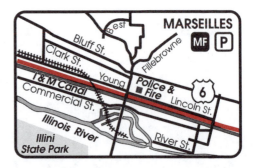

Bicyclists can take advantage of the groomed towpath to enjoy the natural and manmade wonders. The trail is marked and has various wayside exhibits that describe features of the canal era.

The I&M (Illinois and Michigan) Canal provided the first complete water route from the east coast to the Gulf of Mexico by connecting Lake Michigan to the Mississippi River by way of the Illinois River.

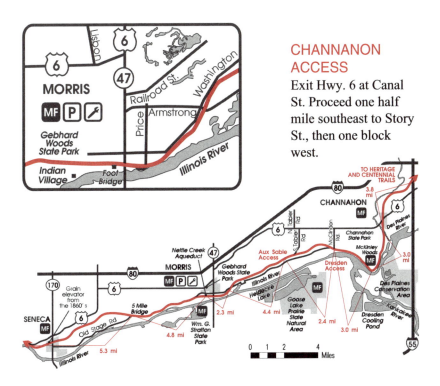

CHANNANON ACCESS
Exit Hwy. 6 at Canal St. Proceed one half mile southeast to Story St., then one block west.

GEBHARD WOODS STATE PARK
Thirty acres of slightly rolling terrain dotted with many stately shade trees.

AUX SABLE
This access area is eight miles from Channahon where an aqueduct, lock and locktender's house can be found.

WILLIAM G. STRATTON STATE PARK
Located in Morris, it provides public boat access to the Illinois River. Picnicking and fishing are popular here.

Goose Lake Prairie State Natural Area

Trail Length	7 miles
Surface	Natural
Information	Goose Lake Prairie State Natural Area 815-942-2899
County	Grundy

Goose Lake Prairie was established in 1969, and covers 2,537 acres of which more than half is a dedicated nature preserve. Goose Lake Prairie is about 50 miles southwest of Chicago and one mile southwest of the confluence of the Kankakee and Des Plaines rivers. This nature preserve contains the largest remnant of prairie ecosystem left in Illinois with the largest stand of tall grass prairie. Grass, flowers, and native plants cover the majority of the park.

While there are no bike paths here, there are 7 miles of hiking trails including a floating bridge. You'll find ample opportunity for viewing the plants and animals that make this area unique. The Tall Grass-Marsh Loop Trail is 3.5 miles. It has a floating bridge that crosses a small lake near its halfway point. This is a self-guiding trek that winds through grasses of big bluestem and Indian grass, which can grow to 8 feet in height. The Prairie View Trail is a 3.5 mile loop of moderate hiking that meanders through the tall grasses to a series of small lakes often visited by waterfowl.

The Visitor Center offers many exhibits, with opportunities to learn about the park through presentations and displays. Be sure to visit Cragg Cabin, a reconstructed cabin from the 1830's that offers a glimpse into the 19th century. Bird watching, picnicking, and wildlife observation are also popular recreational activities among visitors.

Getting There From I-55, take Lorenzo Road/Pine Bluff Road, exit 240, and proceed west approximately 7.5 miles to Jugtown Road. Turn north on Jugtown Road and travel one mile to the entrance on the right side to Goose Lake Prairie State Natural Area, visitor Center, and park trails.

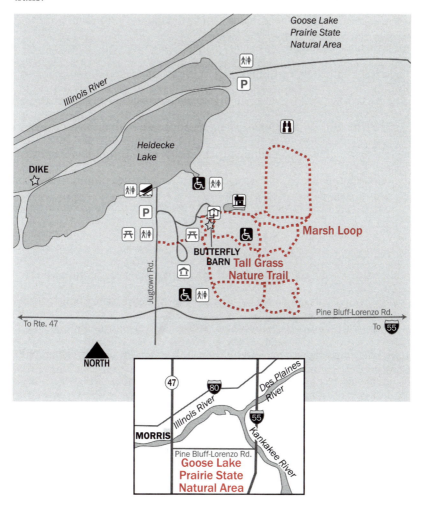

Gebhard Woods State Park

Information   Gebhard Woods State Park   815-942-0796

County   Grundy

Gebhard Woods State Park was established in 1934 and covers 30 acres. The park's information center provides information on the park as well as the I&M Canal State Trail. It is open daily from 10 am to 4 pm. A full time interpreter is on staff to provide educational opportunities to park guests and scheduled groups. Day walks and park programs are scheduled throughout the year. Hikers, campers, picnickers, and canoeists frequent this site, making it one of the state's more popular state parks. Located in Morris, this picturesque park is bordered on the south by the Illinois & Michigan Canal and to the north by Nettle Creek, which gently flows along the perimeter and through the park. Facilities include drinking water, restrooms, picnic areas, shelters, and primitive tent camping. Canoeists can travel 15 miles of the canal in open water between Channahon State Park and Gebhard Woods.

Stately old trees including walnut, oak, ash, maple, sycamore, hawthorn and cottonwood provide ample shade for your visit. In the spring, trillium, bluebell, white trout lily, violets, and spring beauties are some of the wildflowers to be enjoyed. Songbirds, mallards, wood duck, beaver, muskrat, mink, raccoon and an occasional deer also make Gebhard Woods their home.

Getting There   From Route 47 in Morris, turn west on Jefferson Street, which becomes Freemont Street. Continue on Freemont Street to Ottawa Street, and then turn left. The Park is located about a block and a half down of the left hand side.

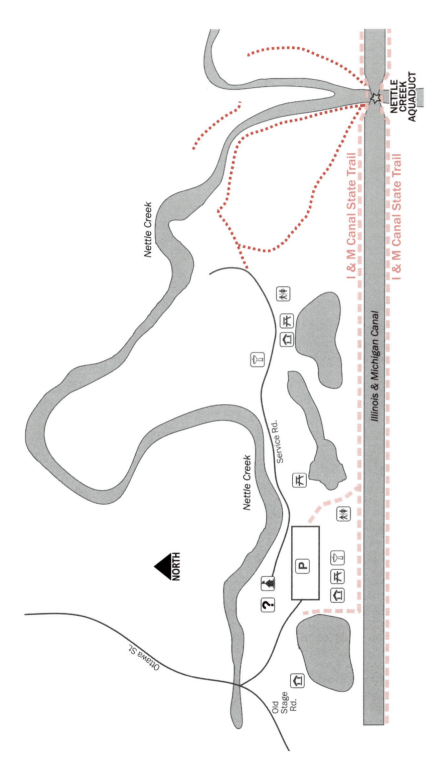

Buffalo Rock State Park

Trail Length	2.5 miles
Surface	Gravel
Information	Buffalo Rock State Park 815-433-2220
County	LaSalle

This 298 acre park is located on a bluff, which was once an island in the Illinois River. This promontory provides a magnificent sweeping view of the Illinois River. The area was the home of the Illinois Indians when Louis Jolliet and Father Jacques Marquette made their trip up the Illinois River in 1673. Later the Illinois Tribe was virtually annihilated in protracted warfare with the aggressive Iroquois. Buffalo Rock served the French as an early military, trading and missionary post. After building Fort St. Louis on Starved Rock during the winter of 1882-1883, almost 4,000 Indian warriors were gathered at the front of Buffalo Rock to form a confederation against the Iroquois. Among the tribes in the confederation were the Miami who built their own fort on Buffalo Rock.

The river Bluff Trail offers a walk high above the Illinois River with two observation decks providing spectacular views of the Illinois River. The Woodland Trail provides an opportunity to observe the trees, plants and wildlife common to the park. The I&M Canal State Trail is located just across the road from Buffalo Rock State Park.

The "Effigy Tumuli" is a tribute to the Native American burial grounds that inspired it. It was the vision of artist Michael Heizer who created the sculptures. It required utilizing heavy equipment on a 1.5 mile long bluff as his canvas. Heizer formed a 2,070 foot-long snake, a 770 foot-long catfish and a 140 foot-long frog, along with a turtle and a water strider. To better appreciate the sculptures, it is best to look first from a distance and then walk around on top of them to better understand the effigies.

There is a small parking area, but water and restroom facilities are not available at this site.

Getting There   From Route 6 in Ottawa, take W.D. Boyce Memorial Drive south to Ottawa Avenue. Turn right and proceed on Ottawa Avenue (which becomes Dee Bennett Road) for approximately three miles. The park is located on the left and the I&M Canal Access area is on the right. From Utica, take Dee Bennett Road east five miles to Buffalo Rock.

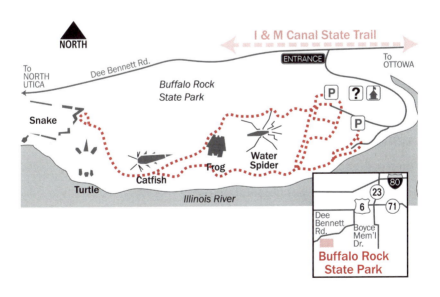

Illini State Park

Trail Length	2 miles
Surface	Packed earth
Information	Illini State Park 815-795-2448
County	LaSalle

This 510 acre park was dedicated in 1935, and is named for the native Americans who once inhabited the area. Illini State Park is located south of the Illinois River from Marseilles and Route 6, and its northern edge is bordered by the Great Falls of the Illinois River. The area is part of an old glacial feature called the Marseilles Moraine and is underlaid by 100 feet of coal. It was heavily mined until World War II. The I&M Canal is located less than a mile north of the park.

Hikers will enjoy exploring the park and its many scenic and historic offerings. Hickory, ash, walnut, elm, cottonwood, oak and maple trees provide shady comfort in the summer and beautiful colors in the fall. Spring is highlighted by blooming wildflowers. Picnic area and shelters with tables, outdoor grills, drinking water, toilets and playgrounds are scattered throughout the park. A concession stand has food and drink in the warmer months. There are both tent and trailer camp sites, and include electric and sanitation service. Some of these sites offer breathtaking view of the river.

Getting There   From Ottawa, take Highway 6 east for 5 miles and follow the signs to the park.

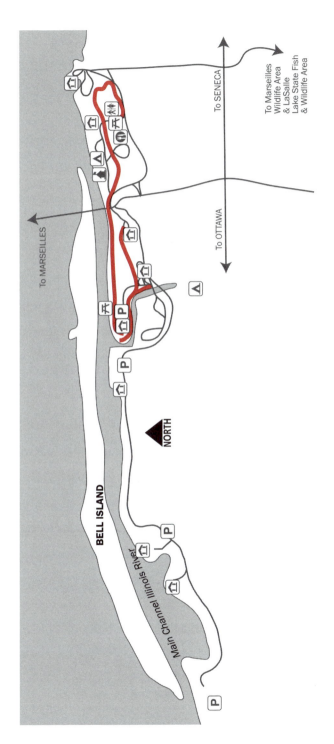

Starved Rock State Park

Trail Length	13 miles
Surface	Natural
Information	Starved Rock State Park 815-667-4726
County	LaSalle

If you enjoy hiking along nature trails, this is the place for viewing the many spectacular overlooks along the Illinois River. Starved Rock State Park, consisting of 2,777 acres, offers 13 miles of well-marked trails, and they are open all year. To keep you oriented, trail maps are located at all trail access points, intersections and points of interest. The color posts correspond to colors on the maps. In addition, yellow dots on trees or posts indicate that you are moving away from the lodge or visitor center, while the white dots mean you are returning. Scheduled guided hikes are available most weekends.

The backdrop for this adventure is the 18 canyons formed by glacial melt water and stream erosion. They slice dramatically through tree-covered, sandstone bluffs for four miles. The park is best known for its fascinating rock formations, primarily St. Peter sandstone, laid down in a huge sandstone in a huge shallow inland sea more than 425 million years ago and later brought to the surface. The areas along the river are predominantly forest, but much of the area is a flat, gently rolling plain.

During early spring and after heavy rains, sparkling waterfalls are common at the heads of the 18 canyons. Some of the longer-lasting waterfalls are found in French, LaSalle and St. Louis canyons. Waterfalls, rivers and streams can undercut a cliff, creating overhangs in the sandstone, like Council Overhang at the east end of the park. The park's lush vegetation supports an abundant wildlife and bird population.

Starved Rock State Park hosts a number of enjoyable annual events, including the Winter Wilderness Weekend in January, the Cross-Country Ski Weekend in February, the Annual Wildflower Pilgrimage in May,

Photo courtesy of Illinois Department of Natural Resources

Starved Rock State Park (continued)

the Montreal Canoe Weekend in June and the Fall Colors Weekend in October. The visitor center is open daily, offering displays and exhibits explaining the park's cultural and natural history. The park has a lodge and restaurant, located on a high bluff just southwest of the rock itself. For reservations, call 800-868-7625.

Photo courtesy of Illinois Department of Natural Resources

Now for a bit of history! In 1673, French explorers Louis Jolliet and Father Jacques Marquette passed through here on their way up the Illinois from the Mississippi River. Known as "Pere", the French word for "Father", Marquette returned two years later to found the Mission of the Immaculate Conception-Illinois, the first Christian mission at the Kaskaskia Indian village. The French built Fort St. Louis atop Starved Rock in the winter of 1682-83, but abandoned the fort by the early 1700's and retreated to what is now Peoria. By 1720 all remains of the fort had disappeared.

Starved Rock State Park derives its name from a Native American legend of injustice and retribution. In the 1760's, Pontiac, chief of the Ottawa tribe, was slain by an Illiniwek while attending a tribal council in southern Illinois. According to the legend, during one of the battles that subsequently occurred to avenge his killing, a band of Illiniwek, under attack by a band of Potawatomi (allies of the Ottawa), sought refuge atop a 125 foot sandstone butte. The Ottawa and Potawatomi surrounded the bluff and held their ground until the hapless Illiniwek died of starvation- giving rise to the name "Starved Rock".

Getting There   Starved Rock State Park is located along the south side of the Illinois River, one mile south of Utica and midway between the cities of LaSalle-Peru, and Ottawa. From I-80, east or west bound, get off at Route 178 (Exit 81), and go south for 3 miles. Follow the signs into the park.

Starved Rock State Park (continued)

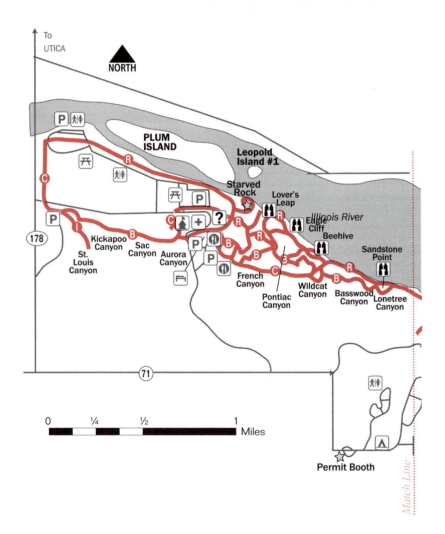

Trails & Canyons

B Bluff Trail – Brown Dots or Post
R River Trail – Red Dots or Post
I Interior Canyon Trail – Green Dots or Post

St. Louis Canyon	1.5 miles
Tonti Canyon	1.9 miles
Starved Rock	0.3 miles
LaSalle Canyon	1.0 miles
French Canyon	0.4 miles
Parkman's Plain	2.5 miles
Lover's Leap	0.7 miles
Hennepin Canyon	3.1 miles
Eagle Cliff	0.8 miles
Ottawa Canyon	3.9 miles
Beehive Overlook	0.9 miles
Council Overhang	4.0 miles
Wildcat Canyon	1.0 miles
Kaskaskia Canyon	4.0 miles
Sandstone Point	1.3 miles
Illinois Canyon	4.7 miles

AREA LEGEND

- City, Town
- Parks, Preserves
- Waterway
- Marsh/Wetland
- Mileage Scale
- Points of Interest
- County/State
- Forest/Woods

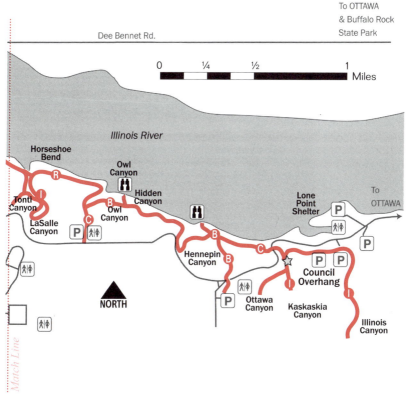

Matthiessen State Park

Trail Length	5 miles
Surface	Gravel, natural - groomed
Information	Matthiessen State Park 815-667-4868
County	LaSalle

Matthiessen State Park features canyons, streams, prairies, and forest. It's located in central LaSalle County, about four miles south of Utica. The many unusual and beautiful rock formations make this 1,938 acre park an educational and fun experience. The Dells Area of the park, with 3.2 miles of trails, has picnic tables, water fountains, toilet facilities, and a large parking lot. An added attraction is the restored fort representative of the fortifications the French built in the Midwest in the 1600s and 1700s. The main trail to the Cascade Falls area originates in this area. The Vermilion River Area to the south has 1.9 miles of trail.

There are five miles of well-marked, well-surfaced hiking trails. Trail maps are located at all major trail intersections. The upper area and bluff tops are easy hiking paths, but the trails into the interiors of the two dells may be difficult to negotiate, particularly during spring and early summer. The trails are rich in animal and plant life, and provide an unparalleled view of geological wonders and you travel through the park.

On the north side of the Dells Area entrance is a parking lot with a hitching post, which marks the access to nine miles of horseback riding trails. Horse rental can be found on Route 71, a half mile west of Route 178. There are also six miles of cross-country ski trails with ski rental available weekends from December through March.

Getting There   From I-80 take Exit 81, Route 178 to Utica, then continue five miles south on Route 178 to the park entrance.

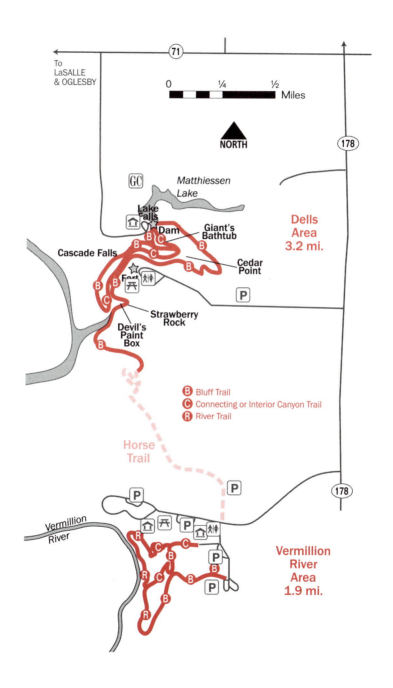

Catlin Park

Trail Length	13 miles
Surface	Packed earth, mowed turf
Information	LaSalle County Parks Dept. 815-434-0518
County	LaSalle

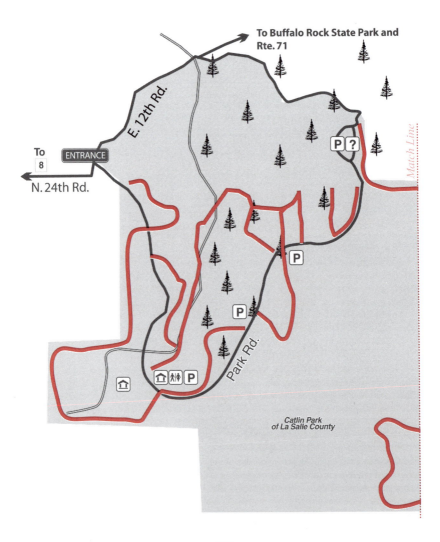

This 333 acre dry habitat park is a mix of bluffland oak-hickory forest, chinquapin oak savanna, maple-basswoods, tallgrass prairie and steep ravines. Catlin Park is basically a modified prairie with open forest that also includes white oak, black hickory, honey locust, and slippery elm. The crisscrossing loop trails travel through all the park's habitats. Facilities include parking areas, picnic shelters, and outdoor restrooms, but there is no drinking water.

Getting There   Catlin Park is located southwest of Ottawa and just east of Starved Rock State Park. From I-80 at Ottawa, take SR 23 (Exit 90) and follow SR 23 south through town and across the Illinois River. Turn right (west) on SR 71 for 2.9 miles, and then left (north) on E. 1251 1st Road. Follow E. 1251 1st Road for 1.2 miles to the park on the left side of the road.

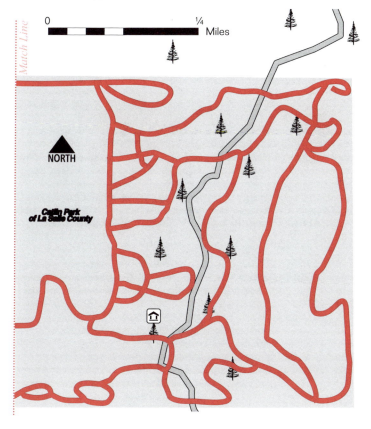

Interconnections — Section 7

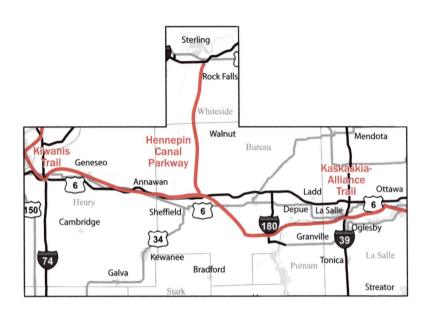

SYMBOL LEGEND

🏖	Beach/Swimming	MF	Multi-Facilities
🚲	Bicycle Repair	P	Parking
🏠	Cabin	⛱	Picnic
⛺	Camping		Ranger Station
🛶	Canoe Launch	🚻	Restrooms
+	First Aid		Shelter
🍴	Food	T	Trailhead
GC	Golf Course		Visitor Center
?	Information		Water
🛏	Lodging	🔭	Overlook/Observation

Grand Illinois Trail

Trail Length	475 miles
Surface	Varies
Information	Illinois Dept. of Conservation 217-782-3715
Counties	Covers 16 counties

The Grand Illinois Trail forms a circular loop from Navy Pier in Chicago past Starved Rock State park to the Mississippi River via the I&M Canal State Trail, the Kaskaskia-Alliance Trail and the Hennepin Canal State Trail. The trail then heads north along the Great River Trail to Savanna and Mississippi Palisades State Park, continues along to Galena then returns to Chicago through other counties bordering Wisconsin.

The Grand Illinois Trail system will eventually contain over 500 miles of rail trails, bike paths, canal towpaths, and greenways along with street routes and lightly traveled town and county roads as it traverses the state. Camping and lodging is available along the way. Trail enthusiasts will be able to enjoy nearby adventure vacations taking on the entire trail in a single effort or more likely completing one segment at a time. In addition to the trails described in this guidebook, the Grand Illinois Trails includes parts of the Fox River Trail, the Illinois Prairie Path, the Prairie Trail, the Des Plaines River Trail, the Robert McClory and Green Bay Trails, and other existing and planned on-and off-road routes.

The Grand Illinois will connect with a national path system, also under development, the 6,300 mile American Discovery Trail. From the

Grand Illinois Trail (continued)

trailhead near the Atlantic Ocean at the Cape Henlopen State Park in Delaware to the Pacific Ocean at the Point Reyes National Seashore in California, the American Discovery Trail will run through urban and remote areas in 15 states and Washington D.C. Through the Midwestern states including Illinois, there will be both a northern and a southern route forming a gigantic 2,500 mile loop from Cincinnati to Denver. It will connect to six national scenic trails and ten national historic trails as well as many regional and local trails systems. You can contact the American Discovery Trail Society at 800-663-2387 for more information.

A series of 17 trails and road segments covering several hundred miles looping Northern Illinois. Some of the proposed route is still conceptual, with linkages to trails via lightly traveled roads and streets.

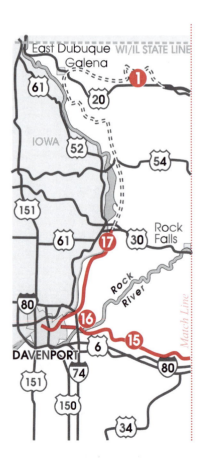

TRAIL LEGEND	
———	Trail-Biking/Multi
············	Skiing only Trail
••••••••	Hiking only Trail
========	Planned Trail
— — — —	Alternate Trail
———	Road/Highway
++++++++	Railroad Tracks

GRAND ILLINOIS TRAIL SYSTEM SEGMENTS

1. Local roads
2. Pecatonica Trail
3. Rockford Area Trails
4. Stone Bridge and Long Prairie Trails
5. Conceptual connection
6. Crystal Lake/Harvard Trail segment
7. Prairie Trail segment
8. Fox River Trail segment
9. Illinois Prairie Path segment
10. Des Plaines River Trail segment
11. Centennial Trail
12. Lockport Historical & Joliet Heritage Trails (& roads)
13. Illinois and Michigan (I & M) Canal State Trail segment
14. Conceptual connection
15. Hennepin Canal State Trail segment
16. Conceptual connection
17. Great River Trail

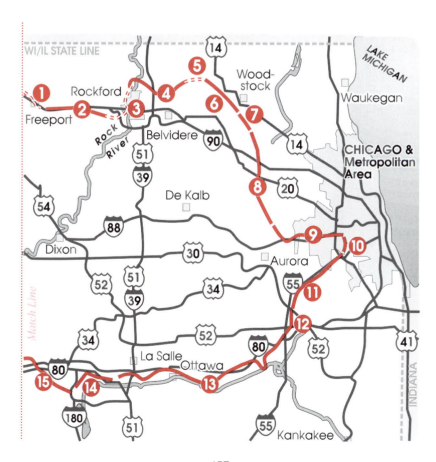

Kaskaskia-Alliance Trail
(under development)

Trail Length	15 miles
Counties	LaSalle, Putnam

This area was once home to the Grand Village of the Kaskaskia, a community of four to six thousand people on the flats across from Starved Rock State Park. The Kaskaskia, as well as other native Illinois tribes, were decimated by the more warlike Iroquois and Algonquin tribes as pressure from American colonists pushed them further west into Illinois territory.

The pursuit of this trail development is to tie together the Illinois & Michigan Canal Trail and the Hennepin Canal Parkway State Trail. The trail will pass through the Illinois Valley communities of LaSalle, Peru, Spring Valley, DePue and Bureau. It follows US Route 6 and local roads between the two canal trails. The Grand Illinois Trail Guidebook, by Todd Volker, is a suggested source of reference for this planned connector trail as well as the Hennepin Canal.

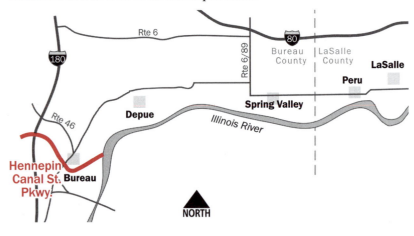

Route from LaSalle:

I&M Canal Lock 14 north to First Street in LaSalle

First Street west to Water Street in Peru

Water Street west to Pike Street

Pike Street north to Main Street

Main Street west to Henry Street

Henry Street north to Fourth Street/Route 6

US Route 6 to Spring valley

US Route 6/Dakota Street west to Dakota Street turnoff

Dakota Street west to Marquette Street

Marquette Street south to Marquette Road

Marquette Road to DePue

Marquette Road/Marquette Street west to Depot Street

Depot Street south to Fourth Street

Fourth Street west to East Street

East Street north to Willow Street

Willow Street west to Illinois Route 29

Illinois Route 29 west to Illinois Route 26

Illinois Route 26 west to Hennepin Canal Lock 3 in Bureau Junction

Hennepin Canal State Parkway

Trail Length	98 miles
Surface	Bituminous – 2 miles, oil & chip 61 miles, gravel – 35 miles
Information	Illinois Dept. of Natural Resources 815-454-2328
Counties	Bureau, Henry, Lee, Rock Island, Whiteside

The Hennepin Canal Parkway is a unique linear waterway corridor in northwestern Illinois. The main line of the waterway extends from the great bend of the Illinois River to the Mississippi River, west of Milan and is a segment of the Grand Illinois Trail.

There are plans to add six miles of trail to connect the Great River Trail along the Mississippi River to the Hennepin Canal Trail.

The western portion of the trail ends at Illinois Route 82 north of Genesseo.

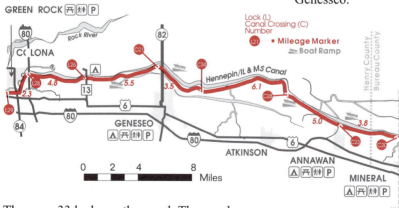

There are 33 locks on the canal. The canal was completed in 1907, but was only used for a short while before being replaced by the railroad.

The parkway is a popular recreational area for pleasure boating, picnicking, primitive camping, horseback riding, snowmobiling, backpacking, and hiking in addition to bicycling. A feeder from the Rock River connects to the main line between Sheffield and Mineral. There are numerous parking areas and road accesses along the parkway.

Day-use facilities consists of picnic tables, pit toilets and parking areas. Most of the areas along the canal have these facilities:

Toilets: Locks 11, 17, 21, 22, 23, 24 and bridges 14, 15, 23 and Visitor Center are have toilet facilities.

Water: Drinking water is available at Locks 21, 22 and the Visitor Center area.

Visitor Center: Includes information, displays, flush toilets, drinking water, playground equipment, picnic areas, boat launching ramp & marina.

The parkway extends south 29.3 miles along the feeder canal. Just north of Interstate 80, midway between Routes 78 and 40, the feeder meets the main canal. From this point the parkway runs southwest 46.9 miles to the Mississippi River near Rock Island and southeast 28.4 miles to the Illinois River near the town of Hennepin.

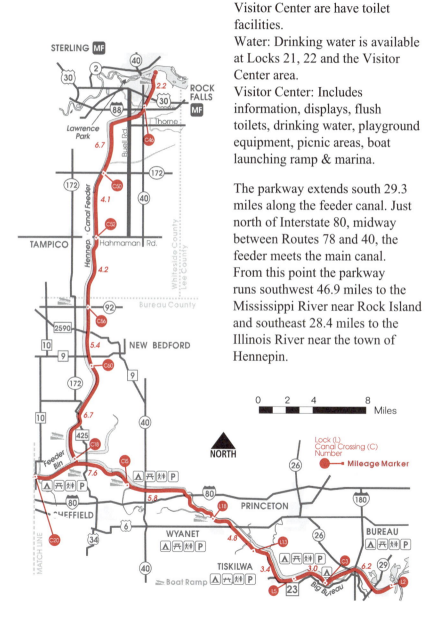

Photo courtesy of Barb Ferry, Forest Preserve District of Will County Volunteer

Find me a place, safe and serene,

away from the terror I see on the screen.

A place where my soul can find some peace,

away from the stress and the pressures released.

A corridor of green not far from my home

for fresh air and exercise, quiet will roam.

Summer has smells that tickle my nose

and fall has the leaves that crunch under my toes.

Beware, comes a person we pass in a while

with a wave and hello and a wide friendly smile.

Recreation trails are the place to be,

to find that safe haven of peace and serenity.

By Beverly Moore, Illinois Trails Conservancy

Visitors Centers

I&M Canal NHC Commission Office
15701 S. Independence Blvd.
Lockport, IL 60441
815-740-2047

Little Red Schoolhouse Nature Center
9800 S. 104th Ave.
Willow Springs, IL 60480
708-839-6897

Isle a la Cacke Museum
501 E. Romeo Road
Romeoville, IL 60440
815-886-1467

I&M Canal Visitor Center
The Gaylord Building
200 W. Eighth St.
Lockport, IL 60441

Will County Historical Society Museum
803 S. State Street
Lockport, IL 60441
815-838-5080

Will-Joliet Bicentennial Park
201 W. Jefferson Street
Joliet, IL 60435
815-740-2216

I&M Canal State Trail-Channahon Access
2 W. Story Street
Channahon, IL 60410
815-476-4271

I&M Canal State Trail
Gebhard Woods Access
102 Ottawa Street
Morris, IL 60450
815-942-0796

Goose Lake Prairie
State Natural Area
5010 N Jugtown Road
Morris, IL 60450
815-942-2899

Buffalo Rock State Park
Information Center
Ottawa, IL 61350
815-433-2224

Illinois Waterway Visitor Center
Route 1, Dee Bennett Road
Ottawa, IL 61350
815-667-4054

Starved Rock State Park
Visitor Center
Utica, IL 61373
815-667-4906

Heritage Corridor Visitors Bureau
Joliet Office
81 N. Chicago Street
Joliet, IL 60432
815-727-2323

Heritage Corridor Visitors Bureau
Utica Office
723 S. Clark Street
Utica, IL 61373
815-667-4356

Heritage Corridor Visitors Bureau
8695 Archer Avenue
Willow Springs, IL 60480
708-839-1322

Accommodations

Hotels, Motels

Countryside
William Tell Holiday Inn
5201 Joliet Road
800-441-6041

Kankakee
Avis Motel
1225 East Court Street
815-933-1717

Economy Inn
1786 State Routes 45 & 52
800-843-5641

Fairview Courts Motel
2745A South US Hwy 45 & 52
815-933-7708

Hilton Garden Inn
455 Riverstone Parkway
815-932-4444

Model Motel
1245 South Washington Avenue
815-932-5013

Marseilles
Prairie Lake Resorts
2550 North 32nd Road
815-795-5107

Morris
Comfort Inn
70 West Gore Road
800-228-5150

Holiday Inn
200 Gore Road
800-HOLIDAY

Park Motel
1923 North Division Street
815-942-1321

Oglesby
Days Inn
120 North Lewis Street
800-329-7466

Holiday Inn Express
900 Holiday Street
800-465-4329

Ottawa
Comfort Inn
510 East Etna Road
800-228-5150

Hampton Inn
4115 Holiday Lane
800-HAMPTON

Holiday Inn Express
120 West Stevenson Road
800-465-4329

Super 8 Motel
500 East Etna Road
800-800-8000

Peru
Comfort Inn
5240 Trompeter Road
800-228-5150

Fairfield Inn
4385 Venture Drive
800-228-2800

La Quinta
4389 Venture Drive
800-531-5900

Super 8 Motel
1851 May Road
800-800-8000

Rock Falls
All Seasons Motel
1904 First Avenue
815-625-3700

Country Inn & Suites
2106 First Avenue
800-456-4000

Holiday Inn
2105 South First Avenue
800-HOLIDAY

Accommodations (continued)

Hotels, Motels (continued)
Super 8 Motel
2100 First Avenue
800-800-8000

Romeoville
Comfort Inn
1235 Lakeview Drive
800-424-5423

Country Inn & Suites
1265 Lakeview Drive
800-456-4000

Super 8 Motel
1301 Marquette Drive
800-800-8000

Shorewood
Joliet Inn
19747 Frontage Road
815-725-2180

Streator
Super 8
7105 North Bloomington Street
815-672-0080

Town & County Inn
2100 North Bloomington Street
815-672-3183

Utica
Grizzly Jack's Grand Bear Lodge
& Waterpark Resort
Route 178
866-399-FUNN

Starved Rock Inn
Hwy 6 & IL Route 178
815-667-4238

Starved Rock Lodge
IL Route 178 & 71
800-868-7625

The Willows
325 Clark Street
815-667-3400

Bed & Breakfasts
Kankakee
River Decks B&B
494 west River Street
815-933-9000

Marseilles
Stain Glass Inn B&B
2820 East 2559 Road
815-795-447

Oswego
Wal-Oak B&B
224 Chicago Road
630-554-9625

Ottawa
Prairie Rivers B&B
121 East Prospect Avenue
815-434-3226

Camping
Channahon
Channahon State Park
2 west Story Street
815-467-4271

Joliet
Empress RV Resort
2300 Empress Drive
888-436-7737

Martin Campground
725 Cherry Hill Road
815-726-3173

River Edge Campground
Khaler Road, 1 mile east
of US Rte 45
815-727-8700

Marseilles
Illini State Park
2660 East 2350th Road
815-795-2448

Troll Hollow Campground
2265 North 2453 Road
815-795-2537

Morris
Gebhard Woods State Park
402 Ottawa Street
815-942-0796

Rock Falls
Leisure Lake Campground
2304 French Street
815-626-0005

Utica
Hickory Hollow
Frontage Road at I-80 and Route 178
815-667-4996

LaSalle Peru KOA Kampground
766 North 3150th Road
815-667-4988

Starved Rock State Park
Illinois Route 178
815-667-4726

Organizations

Bicycling
Chicagoland Bicycle Federation
650 S. Clark Street
Chicago, IL 60605
312-427-3325

League of Illinois Bicyclists
1550 Cheshire Dr.
Aurora, IL 60504
530-978-0583

RIDE
Recreation for Individuals Dedicated to the Environment
208 S. La Salle Street, Suite 1700
Chicago, IL 60604
312-853-2820

Folks on Spokes
PO Box 763
Matteson , IL 60443
708-730-5170

Joliet Bicycle Club
PO Box 2758
Joliet, IL 60436
815-436-3539

Hiking
American Hiking Society
1422 Fenwick Ln.
Silver Spring, MI 20910
800-972-8608

Forest Trails Hiking Club
630-262-1868

Environmental
Forest Preserve District of Will County
17540 N. Laraway Road
Joliet, IL 60433
815-727-8700
fpdwc.org

blue jay

Illinois Trails Conservancy
PO Box 10, 144 W. Main Street
Capron, IL 61012
815-569-2472

Illinois Dept of Natural Resources (DNR)
One Natural Resources Way
Springfield, IL 62702
217-782-6302

Friends of the Lake Katherine Nature Preserve
7402 Lake Katherine Drive
Palos Heights, IL 60463
708-361-1873

Illinois Ornithological Society
PO Box 931
Lake Forest, IL 60045

Midewin Tallgrass Prairie Alliance
30239 S. State Route 53
Wilmington, IL 60481
815-423-6370

The Nature Conservancy
Illinois Field Office
Volunteer Stewardship Office
8 S. Michigan, Suite 900
Chicago, IL 60603
312-580-2100

Save the Prairie Society
10327 Elizabeth
Westchester, IL 60154
708-865-8730

Sierra Club-Illinois Chapter
One N. La Salle Street, Suite 4242
Chicago, IL 60602
312-251-1680

Illinois Audubon Society
PO Box 2418
Danville, IL 61834
217-446-5085

I&M Heritage Corridor Partners
Canal Corridor Association
Dedicated to community economic development, historic preservation and conservation within the Heritage Corridor.
www.canalcor.org

Friends of the I&M Canal National Heritage Corridor
Dedicated to the preservation of the I&M Canal by promoting its maintenance and history.
630-324-1528

Heritage Corridor Convention & Visitors Bureau
Publishes a visitors guide, and packages overnight tours.]
815-727-2323
www.heritagecorridorcvb.com

Illinois and Michigan Canal National Heritage Corridor Civic Center Authority
A State of Illinois agency committed to the historic, recreational, and economic development of communities in the Heritage Corridor.
708-352-4110

Illinois and Michigan Canal National Heritage Corridor Commission
A federal commission serving as a public forum for preservation, conservation, and revitalization of the Heritage Corridor.
815-740-3047
www.dnr.state.il.us

Illinois Dept. of Natural Resources
This state agency owns and manages the I&M Canal and the various state parks within the Heritage Corridor.
815-942-9501
www.dnr.state.il.us/lands/landmgt/parks/i&m /main.htm

Other

American Discovery Trail Society
Northern Illinois Coordinator
816 22nd Street
Rock Island, IL 61201

City to Trail Index

POPULATION CODE
①=under 1,000
②=1,000-4,999
③=5,000-9,999
④=10,000-49,999
⑤=50,000 and over

City Name	Pop.Code	Trail Name
⑤	Bolingbrook	Keepataw Preserve
⑤	Bolingbrook	Veterans Woods
②	Braidwood	Braidwood Dunes & Savanna Nature Preserve
④	Brookfield	Salt Creek F.P. Trail
①	Bureau	Hennepin Canal Parkway
①	Bureau Junction	Kaskaskia-Alliance Trail
③	Channahon	McKinley Woods
③	Channahon	Channahon State Park
③	Channahon	I & M Canal State Trail
⑤	Chicago	Chicago Lakefront Bike Path
②	Colona	Hennepin Canal Parkway
③	Countryside	Arie Crown Bicycle Trail
①	Crete	Goodenow Grove Nature Preserve
④	Darien	Waterfall Glen FP Trail
③	Frankfort	Old Plank Road Trail
③	Frankfort	Hickory Creek Preserve
③	Genesco	Hennepin Canal Parkway
②	Green Rock	Hennepin Canal Parkway
④	Hickory Hills	Palos & Sag Forest Preserve Trails
④	Hinsdale	Salt Creek F.P. Trail
②	Hodgkins	Arie Crown Bicycle Trail
③	Indian Head Pk	Arie Crown Bicycle Trail
⑤	Joliet	Sugar Creek Preserve
⑤	Joliet	Wauponsee Trail
⑤	Joliet	Pilcher Park Nature Center
⑤	Joliet	Old Plank Road Trail
⑤	Joliet	Hammel Woods
⑤	Joliet	Joliet Iron Works Historic Site
⑤	Joliet	Joliet Junction Trail
⑤	Joliet	Will County I&M Canal Trail
⑤	Kankakee	Kankakee River State Park
④	LaGrange	Salt Creek F.P. Trail
④	LaGrange Park	Salt Creek F.P. Trail
③	LaSalle	I & M Canal State Trail
③	LaSalle	Starved Rock State Park
③	LaSalle	Kaskaskia-Alliance Trail
④	Lemont	Lemont's I&M Canal Trail
④	Lemont	Black Partridge Forest Preserve
③	Lockport	Centennial Trail
③	Lockport	Will County I&M Canal Trail
③	Lockport	Messenger Woods
③	Lockport	Lockport Prairie Nature Preserve

③	Lockport	Spring Creek Greenway
③	Lockport	Gaylord Donnelly Canal Trail
③	Lyons	Centennial Trail
②	Marseilles	Illini State Park
②	Marseilles	I & M Canal State Trail
④	Matteson	Old Plank Road Trail
③	Milan	Hennepin Canal Parkway
①	Mineral	Hennepin Canal Parkway
④	Moline	Hennepin Canal Parkway
②	Monee	Monee Reservoir
②	Monee	Raccoon Grove Nature Preserve
④	Morris	Gebhard Woods State Park
④	Morris	I & M Canal State Trail
④	Morris	Goose Lake Prairie State Natural Area
④	New Lenox	Old Plank Road Trail
②	Oglesby	Matthiessen State Park
④	Ottawa	I & M Canal State Trail
④	Ottawa	Buffalo Rock State Park
④	Ottawa	Illini State Park
④	Ottawa	Catlin Park
④	Palos Heights	Lake Katherine Nature Reserve
④	Palos Hills	Palos & Sag Forest Preserve Trails
④	Palos Hills	I & M Canal Trail (Cook Cnty)
②	Palos Park	Palos & Sag Forest Preserve Trails
④	Park Forest	Old Plank Road Trail
④	Park Forest	Thorn Creek Woods Nature Preserve
②	Plainfield	Lake Renwick - Heron Rookery NP
③	Princeton	Hennepin Canal Parkway
③	Rock Falls	Hennepin Canal Parkway
④	Romeoville	Will County I&M Canal Trail
④	Romeoville	O'Hara Woods Nature Preserve
④	Romeoville	Veterans Woods
②	Seneca	I & M Canal State Trail
①	Sheffield	Hennepin Canal Parkway
①	Tampico	Hennepin Canal Parkway
①	Utica	Starved Rock State Park
①	Utica	Matthiessen State Park
④	Westchester	Wolf Road Prairie
④	Westchester	Salt Creek F.P. Trail
④	Western Springs	Salt Creek F.P. Trail
④	Western Springs	Bemis woods
②	Willow Springs	Palos & Sag Forest Preserve Trails
②	Willow Springs	I & M Canal Trail (Cook Cnty)
③	Wilmington	Midewin National Tallgrass Prairie
③	Wilmington	Forsythe Woods
④	Woodridge	Waterfall Glen FP Trail
②	Wyanet	Hennepin Canal Parkway

County to Trail Index

County name	Trail Name
Bureau	Hennepin Canal Parkway
Cook	Bemis woods
Cook	Old Plank Road Trail
Cook	Centennial Trail
Cook	Chicago Lakefront Bike Path
Cook	Black Partridge Forest Preserve
Cook	I & M Canal Trail (Cook Cnty)
Cook	Lake Katherine Nature Reserve
Cook	Wolf Road Prairie
Cook	Palos & Sag Forest Preserve Trails
Cook	Lemont's I&M Canal Trail
Cook	Salt Creek F.P. Trail
Cook	Arie Crown Bicycle Trail
DuPage	Waterfall Glen FP Trail
DuPage	Centennial Trail
Grundy	I & M Canal State Trail
Grundy	Goose Lake Prairie State Natural Area
Grundy	Gebhard Woods State Park
Henry	Hennepin Canal Parkway
LaSalle	Catlin Park
LaSalle	Buffalo Rock State Park
LaSalle	Matthiessen State Park
LaSalle	Starved Rock State Park
LaSalle	Kaskaskia-Alliance Trail
LaSalle	I & M Canal State Trail
LaSalle	Illini State Park
Lee	Hennepin Canal Parkway
Putnam	Kaskaskia-Alliance Trail
Rock Island	Hennepin Canal Parkway
Whiteside	Hennepin Canal Parkway

Will	Sugar Creek Preserve
Will	I & M Canal State Trail
Will	Old Plank Road Trail
Will	Kankakee River State Park
Will	Joliet Iron Works Historic Site
Will	Centennial Trail
Will	Messenger Woods
Will	Channahon State Park
Will	Will County I&M Canal Trail
Will	Lake Renwick - Heron Rookery NP
Will	Joliet Junction Trail
Will	Pilcher Park Nature Center
Will	Midewin National Tallgrass Prairie
Will	Monee Reservoir
Will	Raccoon Grove Nature Preserve
Will	Keepataw Preserve
Will	Spring Creek Greenway
Will	O'Hara Woods Nature Preserve
Will	Hickory Creek Preserve
Will	McKinley Woods
Will	Braidwood Dunes & Savanna Nature Preserve
Will	Forsythe Woods
Will	Wauponsee Trail
Will	Hammel Woods
Will	Veterans Woods
Will	Lockport Prairie Nature Preserve
Will	Gaylord Donnelly Canal Trail
Will	Thorn Creek Woods Nature Preserve
Wll	Goodenow Grove Nature Preserve

Trail Index

Arie Crown Forest Preserve & Trail 36
Bemis Woods 32
Black Partridge Forest Preserve 54
Braidwood Dunes & Savanna Nature Preserve 96
Buffalo Rock State Park 140
Catlin Park 152
Centennial Trail (under development) 72
Central & Eastern Will County 106
Channahon State Park 100
Chicago Lakefront Bike Path 22
Cook County I&M Bicycle Trail 26
Forest Preserve District of Will County Biking Trails 55
Forsythe Woods 98
Gaylord Donnelley Canal Trail 76
Gebhard Woods State Park 138
Goodenow Grove Nature Preserve 122
Goose Lake Prairie State Natural Area 136
Grand Illinois Trail 155
Hammel Woods/Hammel Woods Bikeway 90
Hennepin Canal State Parkway 160
Hickory Creek Preserve/Bikeway East Branch and West Branch 112
Hickory Creek Preserve/Bikeway East Branch 115
Hickory Creek Preserve/Bikeway West Branch 114
I & M Canal Corridor 20
I & M Canal Corridor History 14
I & M Canal Corridor 18
Illini State Park 142
Interconnections 154
Joliet Iron Works Historic Site 86
Kankakee River State Park 104
Kaskaskia-Alliance Trail (under development) 158
Keepataw Preserve 79
Lake Katherine Nature Preserve 44

Lake Renwick – Heron Rookery Nature Preserve 80
Lake Renwick Preserve – Turtle Lake Access/Lake Renwick Bikeway 80
Lemont's I&M Canal Walk Heritage Quarries Recreation Area 51
Lockport Prairie Nature Preserve 84
Matthiessen State Park 150
McKinley Woods 94
Messenger Woods 110
Midewin National Tallgrass Prairie 102
Monee Reservoir 116
Northwestern Will County- 75
O'Hara Woods Nature Preserve 78
Old Plank Road Trail 61
Palos & Sag Valley Forest Preserves 38
Pilcher Park 88
Raccoon Grove Forest Preserve 118
Rock Run Preserve Black Road Access and Nichols Access 68
Rock Run PreserveTheodore Marsh 69
Rock Run Trail & the Joliet Trail Loop 66
Salt Creek Forest Preserve 30
Salt Creek Greenway 28
Southwestern Will County 93
Spring Creek Preserve – Homer Trails 108
Starved Rock State Park 144
Sugar Creek Preserve 92
The Illinois & Michigan Canal State Trail and nearby parks 124
The Illinois and Michigan Canal State Trail 126
Thorn Creek Woods Nature Preserve 120
Veterans Woods 79
Waterfall Glen Forest Preserve 46
Wauponsee Glacial Trail 64
Will County I&M Canal Trail 70
Will County's Linear Trails 58
Wolf Road Prairie 34

American Bike Trails publishes and distributes maps, books and guides for the bicyclist.

For more information:
www.abtrails.com

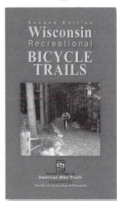